# TRADE AND COMPETITION
# POLICIES FOR TOMORROW

ORGANISATION FOR ECONOMIC CO-OPERATION AND DEVELOPMENT

# ORGANISATION FOR ECONOMIC CO-OPERATION AND DEVELOPMENT

Pursuant to Article 1 of the Convention signed in Paris on 14th December 1960, and which came into force on 30th September 1961, the Organisation for Economic Co-operation and Development (OECD) shall promote policies designed:

- to achieve the highest sustainable economic growth and employment and a rising standard of living in Member countries, while maintaining financial stability, and thus to contribute to the development of the world economy;
- to contribute to sound economic expansion in Member as well as non-member countries in the process of economic development; and
- to contribute to the expansion of world trade on a multilateral, non-discriminatory basis in accordance with international obligations.

The original Member countries of the OECD are Austria, Belgium, Canada, Denmark, France, Germany, Greece, Iceland, Ireland, Italy, Luxembourg, the Netherlands, Norway, Portugal, Spain, Sweden, Switzerland, Turkey, the United Kingdom and the United States. The following countries became Members subsequently through accession at the dates indicated hereafter: Japan (28th April 1964), Finland (28th January 1969), Australia (7th June 1971), New Zealand (29th May 1973), Mexico (18th May 1994), the Czech Republic (21st December 1995), Hungary (7th May 1996), Poland (22nd November 1996) and Korea (12th December 1996). The Commission of the European Communities takes part in the work of the OECD (Article 13 of the OECD Convention).

Publié en français sous le titre :
ÉCHANGES ET CONCURRENCE
Quelles politiques pour demain ?

# FOREWORD

These Working Papers have been prepared, over an extended period, by the OECD Joint Group on Trade and Competition. They draw on OECD's multi-disciplinary approach to economic analysis. The papers are particularly relevant in the lead up to the WTO Ministerial in Seattle at which the question of coherence between trade and competition policy disciplines will be actively discussed. But whatever the outcome at Seattle, the issues raised in these Working Papers point to the need for continuing analysis and policy consideration.

- The paper on Complementarities between Trade and Competition Policies seeks to show that complementarity between the two policies is a key requirement for their effectiveness. In the absence of an effective competition policy, the gains of trade liberalisation may be compromised as a result of restraints on trade by private or public undertakings. Conversely, in the absence of a sustained process of trade liberalisation, the impact of competition policy in promoting the contestability of markets is limited.

- Nonetheless, the paper on Consistencies and Inconsistencies between Trade and Competition Policies suggests that, though mutually supportive, these policies also have their differences. This can reflect the distinct matters dealt with by each policy and the fact that they each have to be co-ordinated with other policy objectives that are the sovereign responsibility of government.

- The paper on Competition and Trade Effects of Vertical Restraints draws as one of its key conclusions the observation that vertical restraints have complex potential pro- and anti-competitive effects. They can also enhance or reduce market access by foreign-based competitors. Accordingly, vertical restraints call for a careful case-by-case, "rule of reason" (i.e. balancing) analysis.

- In looking at Competition Elements in International Trade Agreements, the Joint Group paper suggests that WTO agreements do deal to some extent with the trade and competition interface and considers the question - how far does that coverage actually (or potentially) extend?

- The paper on Implications of the WTO Agreement on Basic Telecommunications (ABT) concludes that the architecture of the ABT provides an interesting case that might warrant closer scrutiny to see whether any of the principles, concepts and approaches might also be applicable to further multilateral rule making in respect of anti-competitive practices that have a significant impact on international trade.

This book is published on the responsibility of the Secretary-General of the OECD.

# TABLE OF CONTENTS

## *Chapter 1*

## COMPLEMENTARITIES BETWEEN TRADE AND COMPETITION POLICIES

## *Chapter 2*

## CONSISTENCIES AND INCONSISTENCIES BETWEEN TRADE AND COMPETITION POLICIES

*Chapter 1*

# COMPLEMENTARITIES BETWEEN TRADE AND COMPETITION POLICIES

## I.    Trade liberalisation: the traditional model of complementarity

Competition policies and trade liberalisation policies are, in general, complementary and mutually reinforcing. Successive rounds of trade negotiations since the end of the Second World War have resulted in dramatic reduction of tariffs world-wide. With the Tokyo and Uruguay Rounds, significant progress has also been made in strengthening and expanding the rules and disciplines needed to ensure that non-tariff measures do not unfairly distort trade. By reducing tariffs and non-tariff barriers to trade, trade liberalisation as embodied through the WTO Agreements creates new export opportunities and spurs international commercial competition, which in turn induces business investment, technological innovation and long-term economic growth. The lowering of tariffs and enhanced competition contribute to lower consumer and input prices, while the consequent expansion of trade will yield higher incomes. In short, the ultimate objectives and outcomes of a successful policy of trade liberalisation will in many instances closely resemble or complement those achieved through the instruments of competition policy.

The reduction or elimination of tariff and non-tariff barriers to trade is perhaps the most natural complementarity between trade and competition policy. This is because, at base, in many respects, competition policy is about protecting consumers from private firms who, unilaterally or collectively, set prices that are higher than would prevail under competitive market conditions. When a firm, acting alone, or together with other firms has the power to raise and sustain price above the competitive level, it has "market power". Firms are unlikely to have market power where entry into the particular market is relatively easy. Tariffs often serve as a barrier to entry by raising prices of otherwise less costly imports. Thus, tariffs may raise prices to consumers, and also make it possible for domestic firms, unilaterally or collectively, to raise prices above the competitive level behind the tariff shield from foreign competition.

Like trade policy, competition policy also attempts to protect consumer interests by dealing with matters that directly affect decision-making by private firms. Trade liberalisation protects consumer interests from sub-optimal firm decision making by increasingly disciplining government activities that inappropriately impede or distort firm decision making from what it would be in open and competitive markets.

Competition law attempts to protect consumer interests from anti-competitive firm decision making by policies and rules that curb the exercise of private market power. Domestic competition laws can be viewed as complementing trade liberalisation agreements by ensuring that the benefits of such agreements are realised and not negated by private restraints to trade. Strong competition in domestic markets also helps to smooth the structural adjustments that arise from trade liberalisation accords. It is therefore critical to the success of trade liberalisation and effective market access that anti-competitive practices be checked through effective competition policies. In short, effective competition policies complement trade liberalisation agreements in the removal of barriers to the competitive process and play an important part in maximising the benefits of trade liberalisation initiatives.

In addition to playing a complementary role to trade liberalisation, competition policy can be an important policy safety net, which can allow countries to reduce direct price and market regulation. Competition law can safeguard the interests of consumers and public welfare and thereby promote political support for regulatory reform.

Consequently, both trade policy and competition policy can be strongly pro-competitive and pro-consumer notwithstanding that one tends to deal with government action "at the border", the other private action "behind the border". In fact, this distinction is not always clear cut in each real-world setting.

## II.     Administrative interaction: examples at work

At the same time, the application of trade policy measures may not always exempt firms from competition law disciplines. This interaction may benefit from an analysis of different circumstances in which trade policy measures may be relevant from a competition policy perspective.

A trade restrictive agreement among domestic and foreign producers may be fully subject to competition law disciplines, even if such an agreement may have been entered into as an alternative to or in order to avoid the possible application of trade policy measures. The enforcement of competition law in such cases is of particular importance, since it limits the risk that domestic producers may use the threat of initiating action under domestic trade remedies law, or otherwise lobbying for protection, in order to induce foreign exporters to enter into unlawful restrictive agreements. It also ensures that trade policy measures may only be taken by public authorities in accordance with domestic procedures and in conformity with WTO obligations.

Competition law may be fully applicable if, following the adoption of a trade policy measure, domestic and/or foreign producers engage in anti-competitive practices, which further restrict trade or have a negative impact on consumer welfare. This would include both agreements and concerted practices among competitors, whether domestic or foreign, as well as possible abuses of a dominant position. The application of competition law, under such circumstances, is an important guarantee to limit any risk that trade policy measures foster an anti-competitive structure in the market or result in non-transparent and permanent restraints on trade flows.

The presence of trade policy measures – as well as other forms of government intervention – may be a factor taken into account in competition analysis, in particular for the definition of the relevant market. Competition authorities may define such a market in national terms if actual or potential import competition is limited as a result of trade measures or other regulatory obstacles. Since this may make it easier to establish the existence of a dominant position in the market, there may be a greater risk for domestic firms of being subject to competition law remedies or of a merger being prohibited by competition authorities. Regulatory obstacles can also result in a more narrow product definition of the market or enhance the restrictive effects of an agreement among firms, such as certain types of vertical restraints (for instance, when government regulation makes it more difficult to set up alternative distribution outlets).

Apart from those instances in which competition law applies, competition authorities can also play a role in the trade policy field through competition advocacy. Such advocacy can take different forms and its specific modalities depend on the domestic legal and institutional framework. In some instances, competition authorities can play a general advocacy role in support of an overall open trade policy stance by highlighting the benefits of such liberalisation for consumer welfare and enhancing the structure of competition in the market. Competition authorities may be directly involved in trade liberalisation and deregulation initiatives, in particular when complementary competition law disciplines are seen as essential to ensure that the benefits of such liberalisation are not negated through anti-competitive practices undertaken by dominant firms. Competition authorities may also be consulted when, within the framework of the application of trade remedies law, issues arise concerning the structure of competition in the market.

A number of examples can illustrate the interaction between trade policy measures and the application of competition law.

Canadian competition law places a great emphasis on actual and potential foreign competition in analysing the competitive effects of a merger. For example, the 1989 acquisition by Asea Brown Boveri Inc. (ABB) of the electric power transmission business of Westinghouse Canada Inc. was approved by the Competition Tribunal. However, the Tribunal required ABB to divest certain assets if ABB was unable to convince the Department of Finance to agree to specific tariff relief measures, including full remission on tariffs on imports of certain large transformers for a five-year period.[1] Upon the expiry of the remission order in 1994, the Director of Investigation and Research, assisted the parties by making representations to the Department of Finance supporting its extension until the end of 1999. The Director concluded that the Remission Order had been effective in maintaining competitive supply conditions for large transformers. It had also allowed new overseas competitors to enter the Canadian market to submit bids and obtain orders from Canadian public utilities. However, the accelerated reduction of tariffs on imports under the then Canada-US Free Trade Agreement did not lead to the anticipated entry of a large US competitor which was expected to become an effective supplier and to replace competition lost as a result of the merger.[2] In the 1990 merger of Canada's two largest flour millers, the parties rejected the Director's initial proposal that the transaction be deferred for six months after the removal of import restrictions on US wheat producers under the then Canada-US Free Trade Agreement to allow factual verification of the degree of US entry. The transaction was abandoned, and subsequent monitoring demonstrated that US flour imports represented less than one percent of 1991 Canadian flour consumption.[3]

In the 10 June 1998 meeting of the Joint Group, the Italian delegate referred to an Italian merger decision between an EC sodium producer and a Bulgarian producer. He noted that the merger would have resulted in a dominant position, but that the Italian competition authority approved it on the condition that the antidumping duty administered at the EC-level was lifted. The Norwegian delegate cited a similar experience in a merger case in the Norwegian flower market. In that case, the Norwegian competition authority concluded that the merger would create a dominant position in Norway, but that a lower customs tariff would permit Swedish flowers to enter the market.[4]

With respect to an aluminium case, the EC condemned an agreement by which the main western aluminium producers agreed to buy certain limited quantities of aluminium from foreign trade organisation of East European countries in exchange for their commitment not to sell to other potential buyers in the Western European market. One of the arguments put forward as a defence by the parties to the anti-competitive agreement was that the restriction was justified since aluminium sales from the foreign trade organisations would have been at dumping prices. The argument was dismissed by the Commission, which stated in its decision: "This argument assumes that private parties may arrogate to themselves public functions. It obscures a clear difference between the regulation of trade by a public authority and regulation by cartels. A public authority must take into account the rights and interests of third parties as well as a general public interest. A cartel is habitually for the benefit of the participants and takes no account of the other two concerns".

With respect to the Soda Ash case, the EC condemned as an abuse of a dominant position a policy of progressive fidelity rebates and supply contracts tying up its major customers undertaken by Solvay, the dominant producer of Soda Ash in part of the Community market. Several aspects of this case are of interest. At the time of the investigation, antidumping duties were in force on US and Eastern European producers. At the same time, the Commission Decision notes that, as a result of changes in exchange parities, Solvay was well aware that US producers could sell in Europe at prices substantially below average EC prices without being guilty of dumping and that the duties were under review. In establishing that Solvay had a dominant position in the market, the application of antidumping duties was one of the factors taken into account by the Commission. Moreover, the Commission found that the effect of the system of progressive rebates applied by Solvay was to make it difficult or impossible for other suppliers to enter the market for the marginal tonnage without selling at unprofitable or dumping prices. The Commission issued a termination order requiring Solvay to abandon its system of fidelity rebates and applied a fine of ECU 20 million.[5]

The Japan Fair Trade Commission (JFTC) passed a recommendation decision ordering four Japanese firms not to decide upon the total quantity of natural soda ash (so-called "trona ash") imports, the price of imports, the allocation rates among firms, or the trading partners for import. After the JFTC's decision, the Japanese market for soda ash apparently changed in the following ways:

(a) An increase in the import of "trona ash", despite the downward trend for the demand of soda ash, and the quantity of imports increased as much as eight times in the four years after the JFTC's decision.

(b) Significant changes in market shares among soda ash manufacturers.

(c) Major increases of the quantity of imports per importer and the number of trading partners of "trona ash".

(d) Rapid and major reductions in the price of soda ash - the price dropped by 20 per cent in the four years after the JFTC's decision.

The JFTC published Guidelines Concerning Distribution Systems and Business Practices in order to prohibit anti-competitive behaviour by the Japanese sole import distribution agent, which pressured the exporter not to sell products to Japanese parallel importers. The JFTC rigorously pursued the elimination of this import-restricting behaviour. For example, in cases such as Hungarian-made porcelain (1994), German-made pianos (1994), and the US-made ice creams (1994), the JFTC judged that actions taken by the sole import distribution agents in Japan to block parallel imports were violating the Anti-Monopoly Act. As a result, parallel imports have now increased.[6]

There are also examples of how these complementarities are addressed in the United States. In the 1994 Pilkington case, the United States Department of Justice (DOJ) charged a British firm and its US subsidiary with monopolising the world-wide flat glass market. The complaint charged that Pilkington entered into unreasonably restrictive licensing arrangements with its likely competitors (including US firms) and, for over three decades, used these arrangements and threats of litigation to prevent US firms from competing to design, build, and operate flat glass plants in other countries, even though Pilkington no longer had enforceable intellectual property rights to warrant such restrictions. The case was settled by a consent decree.[7]

More generally, past work in the Joint Group has explored the power of trade associations, standards setting, conformity assessment and certification bodies to block market access and limit competition. Several US cases, including those involving boilers and pressure vessels and material handling equipment, and a Spanish case involving wire netting used for concrete reinforcement, were discussed.[8] These cases showed that such bodies can have considerable power, both direct and indirect over who competes in a market and that this power has been used to restrain imports, particularly when domestic firms are involved in the decision-making. These cases thus demonstrated a clear complementarity of interest among trade and competition authorities in the operation of such bodies. Moreover, these cases showed that both communities can contribute to the elimination of at least some of the anti-competitive and market-access blocking practices in this area. Clear complementarities emerged in the way both communities could work to eliminate problems posed by both public and private bodies.

In particular, in the area of technical standards and certification, implementation of the TBT agreement was cited as one way trade officials could reduce market access blocking conduct of such bodies, including, in particular, public bodies which might otherwise be beyond the jurisdiction of the competition authorities. (In a number of countries, the actions of government are immune from attack under the competition laws.) The widespread applicability of the TBT agreement is also useful given the great number of bodies with some technical standard-setting or certification responsibility; enforcement actions by the antitrust authorities can deal directly with only a relatively few cases at any one time. Nonetheless, law enforcement actions by competition authorities have been effective in attacking private standards setting and certification bodies which excluded foreign firms. These government enforcement actions should have a deterrent effect on other bodies and can be bolstered by private actions in those jurisdictions which permit them.

## III.    The General Agreement on Trade in Services (GATS) and the basic telecommunications agreement: more recent models of complementarity

The notion that international liberalisation of services needs to be complemented by provisions to protect the openness of a market from potential private anti-competitive practices has been most explicitly recognised in the WTO General Agreement on Trade in Services ("GATS"). With respect to sectors covered in a Member's schedule, Article VIII requires the Member to ensure that a monopoly supplier does not "abuse its monopoly position" when it competes in the supply of services outside its monopoly rights. Article IX(1) provides that "Members recognise that certain business practices of service providers, other than those falling under Article VIII, may restrain competition and thereby restrict trade in services." Article IX obliges Members to accede to any request for consultation with any other Member concerning such practices "with a view to eliminating" them. It also imposes a duty to co-operate in the provision of non-confidential information of relevance to the matter in question.

This was taken even further in the GATS negotiations on basic telecommunications, which were concluded in February 1997. Traditionally, the telecommunications sector has of course been dominated by monopoly suppliers. In many respects, the GATS Agreement on Basic Telecommunication Services is the most explicit example of the mutually reinforcing nature of competition and trade policies in the context of a trade agreement. That agreement addresses both governmental measures and private conduct (albeit in an indirect manner) and addresses both at the border and behind the border concerns using both trade and competition policy instruments and concepts.

Specifically, the Reference Paper to the Agreement contains a general commitment of Members to maintain adequate measures to prevent suppliers unilaterally, or collectively, from engaging in or continuing anti-competitive practices. First, a "major supplier" is defined as one with the power "to materially affect the terms of participation (having regard to price and supply)", either due to control over essential, network facilities or its market position.

In addition, the Reference Paper gives several specific examples of anti-competitive practices. These are:

- Anti-competitive cross-subsidisation.

- Use of information obtained from competitors (with "anti-competitive results").

- Withholding technical and commercially relevant information.

The Reference Paper also applies to "interconnection" issues: e.g. the linking with suppliers providing public telecommunications transport networks or services to allow the users of one supplier to communicate with users of another supplier and to access services provided by another supplier. However, the extent of this obligation is limited to the specific commitments undertaken by a Member. Interconnection must be provided:

(a) under non-discriminatory terms, conditions (including technical standards and specifications) and rates and of a quality no less favourable than that provided for its own like services or for like services of non-affiliated service suppliers or for its subsidiaries or other affiliates;

(b) in a timely fashion, on terms, conditions (including technical standards and specifications) and cost-oriented rates that are transparent, reasonable, having regard to economic feasibility, and sufficiently unbundled so that the supplier need not pay for network components or facilities that it does not require for the service to be provided; and

(c) upon request, at points in addition to the network termination points offered to the majority of users, subject to charges that reflect the cost of construction of necessary additional facilities.

The Reference Paper also builds on transparency in order to ensure that the Agreement can actually be operationalized.  The procedures applicable for interconnection to a major supplier will be made publicly available, and a major supplier must make publicly available either its interconnection agreements or a reference interconnection offer.  With respect to settlement of disputes under the Agreement, the Reference Paper appears to distinguish between disputes about anti-competitive practices and disputes about interconnection.  There is no particular form of dispute settlement provided for disputes over anti-competitive practices of major suppliers.  With respect to interconnection, the Reference Paper indicates that the primary avenue of dispute settlement is to a domestic body.  A service supplier requesting interconnection with a major supplier will have recourse, either "at any time" or "after a reasonable period of time which has been made publicly known" to an independent domestic body, which may be a regulatory body.[9]  That body must be given the authority to resolve disputes regarding appropriate terms, conditions and rates for interconnection within a reasonable period of time, to the extent that these have not been established previously.  It is conceivable that in some countries, the chosen body might not be a regulator, but rather a competition authority.

The Reference Paper also reflects a balance between the objectives of both trade liberalisation and competition policy and other social or policy objectives of interest to governments and civil society.  Article 3 provides that any Member has the right to define the kind of universal service obligation it wishes to maintain, and such obligations will not be regarded as anti-competitive per se.  However, those requirements must be administered in a transparent, non-discriminatory and competitively neutral manner and cannot be more burdensome than necessary for the kind of universal service defined by the Member.  Similarly, any procedures for the allocation and use of scarce resources, including frequencies, numbers and rights of way, must be carried out in an objective, timely, transparent and non-discriminatory manner.

It might be worth asking whether the model of addressing the trade and competition complementarity in the Reference Paper with respect to anti-competitive practices, interconnection, dispute settlement, and balancing other policy objectives could be generalised in other bilateral, regional or multilateral trade agreements. Alternatively, is this a sector-specific model, or are there other sectors to which it conceivably could be applied? Does this Agreement reflect industry-specific technological developments, and/or a broad cross-country consensus on the need for regulatory reform of this particular sector? What doctrinal or regulatory preconditions, if any, are necessary for this model to be successfully replicated?

## IV.        Other bilateral and regional models

There are other bilateral and regional trade agreements that attempt to address proactively, to varying degrees, the complementarity of trade and competition policies. For instance, the Northern American Free Trade Agreement (NAFTA), Chapter 15, contains express provisions relating to monopolies and state enterprises. The NAFTA is a good representative example of the kinds of provisions found in these agreements. It includes provisions ensuring that monopolies: do not infringe the NAFTA in the exercise of any regulatory, administrative or other governmental authority that has been delegated to them; act solely in accordance with commercial considerations in its purchase or sale of the monopoly good or service in the relevant market; provides non-discriminatory treatment to NAFTA investments and investors; does not assert or extend is monopoly position outside the grant of its monopoly power. With respect to state monopolies, the NAFTA commitments are more narrow. Each Party must assure that state enterprises: do not infringe the NAFTA in the exercise of any regulatory, administrative or other governmental authority that has been delegated to them; and accord non-discriminatory treatment in its sale of goods or services. These provisions are subject to the NAFTA state/state (Chapter 20) and investor/state (Chapter 11) dispute settlement provisions.

Delegations might want to consider what lessons can be drawn from the experience the NAFTA and other bilateral and regional models for addressing the complementary objectives of trade and competition policies.

## V.        The role of international competition policy enforcement

Enhanced international co-operation in the competition field could result in significant gains from both the trade and competition policy perspectives. These gains could arise from addressing obstacles to market access arising from anti-competitive practices. This might not only result in an expansion of trade liberalisation and greater security of market access commitments, but also in the more consistent application of competition law as a complement to the process of trade liberalisation.

## Conclusions

From the above, it can be seen that competition and trade policies share a complementary underlying rationale: the elimination or reduction of barriers to, and distortions of, markets. When pursued effectively, trade liberalisation and the application of competition policy are complementary and mutually reinforcing. Trade and competition policy share the common objectives of promoting economic efficiency and welfare and are based on common principles such as transparency, non-discrimination and the need for rule-based economic behaviour. The trade policy objectives of trade liberalisation, non-discrimination and transparency can generally go a long way toward facilitating robust competition in markets. By the same token, the establishment and vigorous enforcement of sound competition laws and competition policies can generally go a long way toward assuring the conditions which are conducive to expanding and sustaining free and open trade among nations. This paper has tried to show that complementarity between the two policies is a key requirement for their effectiveness. In the absence of an effective competition policy, the gains of trade liberalisation may be compromised as a result of restraints on trade by private or public undertakings. Conversely, in the absence of a sustained process of trade liberalisation, the impact of competition policy in promoting the contestability of markets is limited.

# NOTES

1.  The onus is put on the merging parties who are claiming that the merger will not prevent or lessen competition substantially to request the tariff reduction from the Department of Finance. This process usually involves demonstrating that there is broad industry support for the tariff reduction. Requiring the merging parties to make it easier for potential foreign competitors to enter the market (seemingly against their rational self-interest) tends to test the resolve of the merging parties, and their claims that the merger is actually not anti-competitive.

2.  See Industry Canada, *Annual Report Director of Investigation and Research for the Year ended March 31, 1995*, 24, 1996.

3.  See Industry Canada, *Annual Report Director of Investigation and Research for the Year ended March 31, 1992*, 7, 1992.

4.  The Co-Chair cited an Australian case in which the parties to the transaction convinced the competition authority that it would pose no competition problem in Australia. However, in the wake of the merger, the merged firm sought protection from foreign competition. He also cited several examples where Australian firms were able to collude in an environment of import restrictions. The Swedish delegate cited an EC concentration case in which a Swedish firm was found to have a dominant position because in the presence of an antidumping duty the relevant market was defined as an EU market instead of a global market.

5.  These European examples are drawn from the Communication from European Community and its Member States to the Working Group on the Interaction between Trade and Competition Policy dated 7 July 1998, [WT/WGTCP/W/78].

6.  These Japanese examples are drawn from the Communication from Japan to the Working Group on the Interaction between Trade and Competition Policy dated 26 September 1997.

7.  *United States v. Pilkington plc*, 1994-2 Trade Cas. (CCH) ¶70,842 (D.Ariz. 1994).

8.       Drawn from country submissions.

9.       The regulatory body must be separate from, and not accountable to, any supplier of basic telecommunications services, and its decisions of and the procedures used by regulators must be impartial with respect to all market participants.

*Chapter 2*

# CONSISTENCIES AND INCONSISTENCIES BETWEEN TRADE AND COMPETITION POLICIES

## Introduction

This paper addresses the subject of the consistencies and inconsistencies as between the goals and objectives and the means of implementation of trade and competition policies.

The first section of this paper examines at a more general level the broad setting in which both policy domains operate. The second section looks at the objectives of both policies including where there are differences. The third section outlines certain key features relating to the means of application of both policies. The fourth section focuses on certain areas where questions of tangible inconsistency are sometimes claimed to arise. The final section concludes.

## I.     Scope

### *"Border/non border"*

Competition policies and trade liberalisation policies are, in general, mutually reinforcing. Historically, trade negotiations have focused on the liberalisation of "at the border" governmental measures that can or do distort trade flows. In particular, Articles I, II and XXVIII of the General Agreement on Tariffs and Trade (GATT) have, since 1947, provided a framework within which it has proved possible for governments to ratchet down trade barriers through bound reciprocal concessions applied on a most-favoured nation basis. Further, practices most likely to deter trade flows such as quantitative restrictions were subjected to disciplines (such as Article XI) prohibiting them or permitting them subject to a few well-defined exceptions. These at the border issues reflect the traditional "market access" concerns of trade negotiators. Under the GATT, and subsequently the World Trade Organization (WTO), there has also been attention to certain "behind the border" measures that distort or impede trade. The scope of coverage of such measures has steadily expanded over time, most notably in the context of the Tokyo Round and Uruguay Round (see below).

Competition policy has historically focused on assuring competitive conditions "behind the border" because competition laws typically provide jurisdiction to proceed only against anti-competitive effects within the national market. Until relatively recently, competition policies tended to focus on promoting consumer welfare by protecting competition between and among domestic firms, although there are a number of examples, some going back decades, of antitrust enforcement focused on international cartel activity, on domestic conduct which excluded foreign firms and on international mergers. In some cases, extraterritorial assertions of jurisdiction have been controversial. More recently, co-operative enforcement of domestic competition laws has also entered the picture. But, in all cases, the focus is necessarily on the competitive effects behind the border, not at the border, given the jurisdiction of antitrust authorities.

Having made a distinction between the "at the border" emphasis in trade policy and the "behind the border" nature of competition policy, this should not be overdrawn. From the inception of the GATT in 1947, the principle of national treatment embodied in Article III has obliged governments to maintain the conditions of competition between "domestic" and "foreign" goods by proscribing discriminatory application of governmental measures such as internal taxes and certain other national laws and regulations.

Similarly, while "domestic" subsidies that could affect competition behind the border (or in third markets for that matter) were not prohibited outright within the GATT system, they have been subjected to disciplines that aim at curbing their trade distortive effects, e.g. via countervailing measures at the border or by resort to multilateral dispute settlement. This framework has been further refined with the creation of the WTO in 1994 and the adoption of the Agreement on Subsidies and Countervailing Measures.

It may be noted that some (but not all) competition policy regimes are also concerned with the competitive effects of state aids and other forms of subsidies. The addition of WTO disciplines on Services, Trade Related Investment Measures (TRIMs), and Trade Related Aspects of Intellectual Property Rights (TRIPs) also evidences the increasing attention being paid by trade negotiators to behind the border measures. With respect to competition policy, globalisation has contributed to a heightened awareness about the effect of residual border measures such as tariffs and other forms of duties that might distort conditions of domestic competition.

### *Public/private*

A perhaps more fundamental distinction to be conscious of when examining the two policy domains relates to public versus private conduct. The GATT of 1947 focused predominantly on governmental measures - either at the border in the form of quantitative restrictions and tariffs or behind the border in the form of discriminatory laws and regulations. Furthermore, with respect to state trading enterprises, the GATT/WTO framework has always dealt with the actions of such enterprises when engaged in "market" functions. Trade distortions from such actions - whether through public procurement or other market behaviour - have been subjected to discipline. Certain private conduct (such as "injurious sales below normal value") was dealt with directly under, e.g. anti-dumping disciplines.

With the creation of the WTO, the trade regime has broadened the scope of its application to certain private conduct relating to, e.g. safeguards (with respect to voluntary restraint agreements), services and intellectual property. While national competition policies are not uniform in this regard, it is arguable that, historically, competition policy has tended to be applied more broadly to private conduct rather than governmental conduct (as a function of the sovereign immunity and act of state legal doctrines). More recently, competition policies are reaching into governmental conduct in the area of regulations covering essential facilities and professional services, in addition to public utilities and state or regulated monopolies either through the direct application of positive law or through competition advocacy.

In many respects the GATS Agreement on Basic Telecommunication Services is the best example of the mutually reinforcing objectives of competition and trade policies. That agreement addresses both governmental measures and private conduct (albeit in an indirect manner) and addresses both at the border and behind the border concerns using both trade and competition policy instruments and concepts.

## II. Objectives

From the above, it can be seen that competition and trade policies share a broadly compatible underlying rationale: the elimination or reduction of barriers to, and distortions of, markets. The importance of having such a mutually reinforcing nature of policies is perhaps best revealed when it is not present. The absence of a national competition policy can deter or prevent access to foreign goods at lowest cost. Similarly, the absence of trade and investment liberalisation deters or prevents access to pro-competitive foreign goods or producers. Both policies are based, at least in part, on the recognition that a market without distortions maximises efficiency and allocation of resources within the economy. That being said, it is worth (a) discussing the concept of "efficiency" more fully, and (b) noting the presence of policy considerations that temper that perspective.

## *Efficiency objectives*

The economics of competition policy and trade liberalisation are often quite similar. Competition policy is concerned first and foremost with economic efficiency, composed of allocative, productive and dynamic efficiency. Allocative efficiency is concerned with ensuring that economic resources are distributed to those who put the greatest value on them. This is efficiency in exchange. Productive efficiency is concerned with assuring that a given level of output is achieved at the lowest cost. In competitive markets, both allocative and productive efficiency are achieved at the same point. While allocative and productive efficiencies are static concepts, dynamic efficiency is concerned with the process of discovering the best technologies, processes and products for meeting changing consumer tastes and incorporating them efficiently into the economic system.

Trade liberalisation policy similarly may be oriented towards all three of these objectives. Removing tariff, non-tariff and internally based barriers to trade through negotiated concessions are the principal means of achieving the allocative and productive efficiency objectives.

Competition policy is also concerned with distortions of competitive market conditions caused by predatory practices of dominant firms that may lead to the exclusion or foreclosure of smaller firms from the market and harm competition. Similarly, trade policy is concerned, on the one hand, with practices of firms that impede access for exports to the market concerned. On the other hand, it also provides for certain counter measures in response to sales below normal value determined to be injurious to a domestic industry.

24

## Broader context

Notwithstanding this broad convergence, it is a simple matter of fact that both policy domains operate in a broader context where other public policy objectives need to be co-ordinated and prioritised by sovereign governments.

In the case of trade policy this is reflected in a number of areas, such as (for instance) provisions that permit departures from "liberalisation" approaches in order to implement measures necessary to protect human, animal or plant life or health, conservation of exhaustible natural resources or measures considered necessary to protect essential security interests. Clearly, to the extent of liberalisation in some cases reflects the outcome of a balancing of public policy objectives relating, e.g. to sustainable development, environment and employment. In areas such as trade in agriculture where trade restrictions have been historically high, this has reflected *inter alia* complex national, social and environment policy objectives. Nor is this fundamentally different in the case of competition law and policy. For instance, in the case of certain sectoral exclusions (and agriculture would be one of these) this reflects a public policy response to broader policy implications as is the case with trade policy.

## Different emphasis

The two policies can also have somewhat differing perspectives. The underlying rationale of multilaterally-based trade liberalisation is generally to set terms and conditions at the international level which will be compatible with global consumer welfare and achieving global productive efficiency. It requires, of course, agreement of sovereign governments to get closer to that objective and, as a consequence, it is a "work in progress". That is one reason why the MFN principle has been such a vital component of the GATT-WTO system. Competition analysis has, by comparison, been more particularly focused on consumer welfare in relation to a class of consumers in a defined market.

At the risk of some over-simplification, it can still be said that, while both policies are concerned with micro economic issues, competition policy emphasises a fact specific, case by case approach, and is usually applied *ex post* (although merger review is an exception), while trade policy often involves more of a sectoral or economy-wide approach and is usually applied *ex ante* (although trade remedies are an exception). Similarly, competition policy often emphasises issues of actual competition in particular markets, while trade policy often focuses on issues of potential competition in the sense of safeguarding competitive opportunities. This may lead, for instance, to a broader definition of markets in trade policy terms than in competition policy analysis. It may also mean that competition policy sometimes appears to have a concern for short-term effects while trade policy has more of a concern for long-term market effects. These differences may have implications for the means and mechanisms employed by both policies as discussed below.

### III.    Means/Mechanisms

*Key practices*

When competition policy is pursuing its allocative and productive efficiency objectives, it is often concerned with concerted efforts to raise prices artificially above competitive levels. This is the reason for the emphasis on proscribing horizontal agreements to fix prices among competitors, or a number of other practices that have the same effect such as bid rigging, market allocation, etc. With regard to certain other forms of horizontal co-operation, all types of efficiency considerations - productive, allocative and dynamic - apply. These may support acceptance of such types of horizontal co-operation, including various types of joint ventures and other consortia. The concern for efficiency also gives rise to the review of mergers between or among competitors that might lead to increased price or less innovation, and hence a reduction in consumer welfare.

In competition policy, the efficiency objective increasingly provides the framework for assessing vertical relationships.[1] Such relationships can include contractual provisions such as exclusive dealing, exclusive territories, tie-ins, and so forth. Here, a complex analysis is needed which may involve examining a reduction in intrabrand competition in conjunction with positive and negative effects on interbrand competition, some of which may arise only over time. Likewise, efficiency concerns motivate control of conduct by dominant firms, particularly conduct which excludes or forecloses competitors from a market by means other than vigorous competition. Such conduct could include the kinds of vertical restraints cited above and also extends to unilateral conduct such as predatory pricing or refusing to deal. The important point for this note is that all jurisdictions provide in some way for sanctioning such abusive conduct through administrative or civil procedures. In some jurisdictions, competition policy is empowered to address this abusive conduct whether performed by private or governmental entities.

In terms of trade policy, removing tariff and principal non-tariff barriers to trade whether autonomously or through negotiated concessions is the means of fostering the allocative and productive efficiency objectives. This approach can either be focused on particular products or sectors, or can be pursued through broad general measures. For instance, a tariff negotiation that results in a lowered bound tariff rate for a particular product might lower the price to consumers as well as the cost of production to other producers for whom the product is an important input. Similarly, trade negotiations that open particular service sectors to foreign suppliers might reduce prices to consumers and costs accordingly.

In the case of goods, trade policy also works through rules-based disciplines such as national treatment (GATT Article III), most-favoured nation (MFN - GATT Article I), and general elimination of quantitative restrictions (GATT Article XI). These obligations have the effect of ensuring that reductions in protection (via the MFN principle) expose the market concerned to (global) least-cost sources. National treatment may serve both objectives by assuring that foreign goods or (as the case may be) service providers receive no less favourable regulatory treatment than domestic goods or service providers.

Trade policy manifests a concern for market exclusion and foreclosure in a number of ways. For instance, exclusion might be addressed by negotiated rights of market access obtained in the form of reciprocal trade concessions. The February 1997 GATS Agreement on Basic Telecoms might provide a good example of this. Exclusion might also be dealt with by the application of national treatment principles to governmental measures that would otherwise have the effect of restricting market access. It is important to stress, however, that where trade policy addresses these issues, it frequently does so in a negotiated and progressive manner, as opposed to the case by case approach of domestic competition policy enforcement.

### Structural resemblance

It also may be worth noting certain "structural" similarities across the policy domains. For instance, both competition and trade policies recognise a limited class of conduct that is impermissible or *per se* illegal. In the trade policy world, the prohibition on the use of quantitative restrictions in GATT Article XI is a fairly broad prohibition. Furthermore, the Uruguay Round Multilateral Agreement on Safeguards provides for the elimination of voluntary export restraints (VERs), orderly marketing arrangements or any other similar measures on the export or import side (including compulsory import cartels and discretionary export and import licensing schemes any of which afford protection). In many jurisdictions, abstracting from associated definitional problems, competition policy would recognise a class of "hard core" cartels without any redeeming efficiency justification to be per se illegal. For conduct that does not fall within the limited class of per se illegal acts, both competition and trade policy rely to a large extent on detailed factual analysis that may be conducted in administrative or judicial settings. We will discuss below how these settings may differ in respect of certain practices and procedures.

### Institutional arrangements

The institutional mechanisms for enforcing competition policy reflect the particularities and heritage of each jurisdiction's administrative and judicial systems. Accordingly, in some jurisdictions, enforcement remains subject to a political override. In others, enforcement is administered to varying degrees by independent authorities. Elsewhere, enforcement is a mixture of the two. In some jurisdictions, enforcement is before administrative agencies and only secondarily by courts, while in others the courts and the administrative agencies can provide primary avenues for redress. In the latter case, private rights of action are available to enable private parties to bring their claims. In some jurisdictions, the remedies are of an administrative nature and involve only fines or fines combined with findings of nullity, while in others remedies can involve civil or criminal fines, prison terms, and injunctions. In an increasing number of jurisdictions, administrative guidance, enforcement guidelines and advisory opinions are used in enforcement policy.

Trade policy is likewise implemented by a range of institutions. Liberalisation is often unilateral, being the product of a co-ordinated inter-agency process under ministerial authority. In some cases, it is undertaken as part of a regional liberalisation arrangement involving intergovernmental negotiation. At other times, it can be the outcome of a multilateral negotiation. In all cases, it is an essentially political process entered into by governments. However, its status in domestic law/regulation, etc. is complex. Depending on the country concerned, there will be a combination of administrative agencies, political institutions, and courts involved. Unlike the case with competition policy, trade commitments are also increasingly subject to binding negotiated multilateral rules. Any breach of such intergovernmental agreements may entitle affected state parties to have recourse to counter-measures pursuant to the relevant (e.g. WTO) international agreements.

Given the wide variance in institutions in both domains, it is difficult to comment usefully about where these particular differences between the trade and competition institutions give rise to what might be described as "inconsistencies".

## IV. What counts as an "inconsistency"?

In the above sections of the paper an attempt has been made to make a first, albeit non-exhaustive, overview diagnosis of a number of the possible areas where there appear to be manifest similarities, complementarities, divergences or differences in the policy domains.

But these, in and of themselves, do not necessarily mean that there are "inconsistencies" in the sense that one policy domain impedes or conflicts with the operation of the other. The latter consideration is presumably the more important issue to focus on inasmuch as it has a practical bearing.

It must be said in this context that many of the issues highlighted in the text above may not give rise to practical inconsistencies. The differences relate to differences of objectives or policy domains which mean that effective implementation of one policy has no particularly damaging implication for the other. Of course, the reality of integrating markets has meant that the question of whether there are consistencies or inconsistencies is all the more important - not just from a viewpoint which is concerned to avoid conflict but also from a perspective which is concerned to maximise policy coherence.

With that in mind, the following issues are a first attempt to focus in on some areas where some have held that there may be more practical consistency questions at issue:

- As noted above, trade liberalisation involves opening particular markets through reductions in tariff and non-tariff barriers. In certain cases, this liberalisation is consolidated in the form of binding commitments at the multilateral level. How significant a problem is it that certain exclusions from the application of domestic competition policies exist? If it is considered to be a problem as far as consistency is concerned, is this a matter to be seen as principally (a) an area where there is a prospect for new and improved market access as a result of changes to application of competition law; and/or (b) an area where existing commitments are in fact being undermined and legitimate expectations frustrated?

- Many jurisdictions continue to except export cartels from anti-trust laws. Is there a shared view that such cartels generally increase prices to foreign consumers or otherwise facilitate anti-competitive practices to the detriment of foreign consumers?[2] If so, does this raise issues of consistency as between trade and competition policies? Is there any possibility that measures to deal with such

29

practices by either trade and/or competition policies could lead to conflicting outcomes?

- In the area of governmental monopolies or entities granted exclusive or special privileges, is there any reason to believe that the respective discipline of international trade rules and competition laws could lead to conflict? Alternatively, is there scope for making these policies work in a more coherent fashion to meet objectives shared by both policy communities?

- Is there any reason to believe that the pursuit of bilateral co-operation or positive comity agreements raises any problem of consistency as far as international trade obligations are concerned? Is there satisfaction that such arrangements are compatible with the national treatment and MFN obligations under the WTO?

- What are the residual border trade measures that create inconsistencies for national competition policies? Are there salient sectors where application of governmental measures at the border materially interferes with the attainment of competition law implementation?

- Is it considered that there is an inconsistency in the way in which trade remedies are applied under trade law and the way in which competition law and policy deals with predation and low cost pricing? If so, are there relevant differences in the policy objectives in each domain that account for this?

- Is there any reason to believe that competition policy, when applied in practice to, e.g. vertical restraints, can adopt a perspective based on net efficiency gains to the domestic economy that is inconsistent with a trade perspective that seeks to account for efficiency effects on the "foreign" or global market? If so, is this an inconsistency that is more theoretical than real? Is it also an inconsistency that relates specifically to the maintenance of negotiated multilateral trade commitments?

- Is there any reason to believe that the manner in which competition law applies to standards setting bodies or professional licensing associations can create inconsistencies with rights and obligations under international trade agreements and vice versa?

**Conclusions**

This paper has sought to provide an overview of various possible consistencies and inconsistencies between the trade and competition policy domains. For the most part, we found that both policies are broadly compatible or at least mutually supportive. However, they also have their differences. In some cases this reflects the distinct matters dealt with by each policy. In others, it reflects the fact that either (or both) have to play their part in - and be co-ordinated with - other policy objectives that are the sovereign responsibility of governments. This may lead to differences of perspective or approach. We also noted that there are resemblances in the policy instruments and institutions employed in the discharge of their functions, although the wide variance made it difficult to draw firm conclusions here.

It appears important to stress that even where differences in application of the two policies arise, it is not yet altogether clear as to how much these differences actually impede the operation of one or the other policy.

It is suggested that a practical orientation might, in the future, focus more narrowly on defining where such potential inconsistencies may or may not arise. The questions outlined above are a first attempt to identify possible candidates. The aim of such an approach would be to avoid any temptation to pursue an unduly academic or abstract discussion. Rather, the object would be to see whether there is some tangible and substantive problem that needs to be dealt with. This, it is suggested, may be the most appropriate next step to take by way of elaboration.

*Addendum*

# ELABORATION OF CERTAIN ELEMENTS RELATING TO TRADE REMEDIES AND INTELLECTUAL PROPERTY ISSUES

## Trade remedies

To simplify the analysis here, this section considers only two trade remedies. In particular, it considers safeguard measures and antidumping, and compares aspects of them with two types of prohibition found in competition laws - the prohibition against price discrimination and the prohibition against predatory pricing. It begins with a discussion of the various objectives of trade remedy laws, followed by a discussion of market definition; a discussion of the way in which price discrimination is addressed under trade and competition law; a comparison of the ways in which issues of price predation are addressed under trade and competition law; a comparison of how "injury" is determined in trade law with proof of anti-competitive effect in competition policy; and finally, a discussion of procedures and remedies.

### *Objectives of trade remedy laws*

There are three principal forms of trade remedy laws: antidumping; subsidies and countervailing duties; and safeguards. In this Section we focus on two of these - antidumping and safeguards.

The WTO Agreement on Safeguards permits Members to apply such measures where a product is being imported into its territory in such increased quantities under conditions that cause or threaten to cause "serious injury" to a domestic industry. These measures are subject to strict disciplines and time-limits, and may only be applied to the extent necessary to prevent or remedy the serious injury. For the purposes of this paper, perhaps the most significant aspect of the WTO Agreement on Safeguards is the complementarity between trade and competition policy with respect to certain prohibited measures. Article 11 provides that Members shall not seek, take or maintain any voluntary export restraint, orderly marketing arrangements or any other similar measures on the export or import side. Footnote 4 to the Agreement further provides that examples of similar measures include: export moderation; export-price or import-price monitoring systems; export or import surveillance; compulsory import cartels and discretionary export or import licensing schemes, any of which affords protection.

It is useful to keep in mind that, in the evolution of GATT/WTO practice and various national trade laws, there has tended to be a link between evolution of policies with respect to antidumping and those that address issues of safeguards. On this "realpolitic" view, the antidumping laws represent a continuing belief by governments that the task of trade and investment liberalisation and market integration is still incomplete. Accordingly, governments retain a rules-based way to protect their domestic industries from unfair or injurious trade practices that arise from the incomplete nature of trade and investment liberalisation to date despite the substantial progress made over the last fifty years. Viewed in this way, antidumping laws are not primarily concerned with issues of anti-competitive price discrimination, predation or exclusion and their consequent effects on consumer welfare in the short-term. Rather, antidumping laws are a disciplined way, subject to binding multilateral agreement, to ensure that the competitive conditions between and among domestic and foreign goods and firms are safeguarded in such a way that the political consensus for trade and investment liberalisation with its consequent positive effects on consumer welfare in the longer term can be maintained.

### Market definition

Competition law focuses on effects on competition, and on particular buyers, rather than effects on particular firms. Effects on competition of particular practices are assessed within a "relevant" product market, which is defined based on buyers' demonstrated ability and willingness to substitute between or among a range of similar products and their suppliers. In that sense, market definition is a crucial and technical exercise for the application of competition law.

Trade policy is not necessarily concerned with effects on a "competitive" range of products. This reflects the fact that negotiated tariff concessions are the outcome of a politically negotiated process in which governments "trade" reductions in certain products for reciprocal tariff reductions in certain classes of foreign products. There is no in-built requirement that the MFN or national treatment principles apply across a range of "competitive" products *per se*. It can be a question of whether there has been a commitment by a government to grant particular treatment to a partner's product listed in the tariff schedule. Even if the tariff concession related to a product falling into the same line of the Harmonised Tariff Schedule, it is not necessarily the case that all competing products within that HS classification would receive similar treatment. The government concerned may have chosen to grant different tariff treatment to a specific sub-category. However, there are situations where certain conditions of competition, including demand substitution issues, enter into consideration (see for instance, recent WTO cases relating to Article III). In antidumping and countervailing duty investigations, to some degree demand substitutability is factored into determinations of the "like product" for antidumping and countervailing duty determinations and "domestic injury" for material injury determinations.

The reciprocal negotiated concessions have depended very heavily for their effectiveness on consistency and predictability of treatment. It would be difficult to operationalise the *ex post* market definition of competition policy for the ex ante negotiating purposes of trade policy.

### Antidumping and price discrimination

At this point it is worth noting that the potential for dumping can be facilitated by market segmentation caused, for example, by tariff barriers or as a result of other obstacles such as norms, standards testing procedures, closed distribution systems or insufficient operation of anti-trust legislation in the exporting country. Without such restrictions or distortions, price differences with other markets should be narrowed because of import competition. Where active import competition takes place in a market, exporting from that market at dumped prices does not normally make sense, as at least part of the low priced goods would be re-exported to the country of origin with the consequence of price arbitrage which would negatively affect the exporter's domestic business. For this reason, the parties to some free trade agreements have agreed to curtail or abolish the antidumping trade remedy. Market segmentation, by contrast, gives exporters scope to maintain higher prices on their home market and thus to compensate lower export prices.[3]

Antidumping laws are primarily directed at international price discrimination. In such cases, there appears to be at least broad resemblance between injury under antidumping laws and "primary line"[4] injury under competition laws concerning price discrimination. However, price discrimination claims in a domestic context in some (but not all) jurisdictions must be shown to harm competition (a topic discussed in more detail below), not merely to harm particular competitors. Furthermore, in some jurisdictions a complaint of price discrimination is subject to defences such as "meeting the competition", i.e. when a competitor lowers his price in one area in order to compete with the lower prevailing price in that area.    There is no similar defence available in dumping cases.


## *Antidumping and predatory pricing*

In some countries' views, antidumping laws are essentially concerned with issues of predation, leading to a comparison of the standards of proof under trade and competition laws.[5]    However, in some other countries' views, antidumping laws are not concerned with issues of predation.    Be that as it may, in most jurisdictions, competition authorities use some proxy for marginal costs such as average variable cost in determining whether predatory pricing is involved.    On this view, the notion of predation is less strict.    Predation in the antidumping context is not directly linked to any cost standard, except where constructed costs are involved in which case some proxy for average total cost is used.    Indeed, dumping laws are primarily directed at international price discrimination, not price predation *per se*.    It is worth noting that neither Article VI of GATT 1994 nor the WTO Antidumping Agreement make any reference to predation.

In addition, as discussed below, there are significant differences between antidumping and predatory pricing in terms of the requirements of injury and anti-competitive effects.


## *Determination of injury and anti-competitive effects*

A key component of antidumping analysis is an assessment of material injury to the domestic industry.    With respect to price discrimination and predation, competition law in most countries involves a consideration of the competitive effects of the practice under investigation.

That being said, the question of price predation under competition law is generally not reached unless some type of market power screen has been passed.    That is, unless market structure and entry conditions create a real risk of successful predation, i.e. an anti-competitive effect that reduces consumer welfare, there is no need to enter into complex cost calculations.

On the other hand, antidumping laws are concerned with the impact of "dumped" imports on the domestic industry.    In making that determination, the WTO Agreement on Implementation of Article VI of the General Agreement on

Tariffs and Trade 1994 requires a consideration of "all relevant economic factors and indices having a bearing on the state of the industry, including actual and potential decline in sales, profits, output, market share, productivity, return on investments, or utilisation of capacity; factors affecting domestic prices; the magnitude of the margin of dumping; actual and potential negative effects on cash flow, inventories, employment, wages, growth, ability to raise capital or investments." Under the WTO rules, the determination of injury is a separate inquiry from the determination of dumping margins. When injury cannot be proven, the analysis ends regardless of whether the existence of a dumping margin has been proven. Furthermore, the WTO rules provide that there "shall be immediate termination in cases where the authorities determine that the margin of dumping is *de minimis* [less than 2% of the export price], or that the volume of dumped imports [generally less than 3% for any one country], actual or potential, or the injury, is negligible."

Apart from the limited class of cases that various jurisdictions proscribe as *per se* illegal in their domestic competition policy, competition enforcement usually requires some proof of injury before a remedy is imposed. In the trade context, the GATT-WTO framework requires that authorities examine any known factors other than the dumped imports which at the same time are injuring the domestic industry, and injuries caused by these factors must not be attributed to dumped imports. It is worth noting that both the EU and Canada have legislative provisions that provide for public interest concerns to be factored into the decision whether to apply an antidumping or countervailing duty. The "Community interest rule" means that before taking a decision on antidumping measures an overall estimation shall be made of all the interests pro and against such measures so that account shall be taken not only of the interests of the EU producers but also of the interests of the user industry (and the consumers within the EU if the product under investigation is a final consumer item).[6]


*Procedures and remedies*

In jurisdictions where fines for competition violations are limited to offsetting rather than punitive damages, it would appear to be difficult to distinguish between the two approaches to injury determination, except that, as indicated above, in competition cases there must generally be proof of injury to competition as well as proof of injury to particular firms.[7] In both cases, however, it would be important to assess actual practice before making any sweeping comparisons.

The interrelationship between trade and competition policy remedies is complex in that the use of one policy remedy might have an effect on the necessity of the other remedy. For instance, a number of otherwise anti-competitive mergers may be approved conditional on the lifting of existing trade remedies such that price competition to the merged firm might be provided by increased import competition. Also, it is possible that where price undertakings are used as an antidumping remedy there might be an inconsistency where competition policy might otherwise view such arrangements as hard core cartels. Voluntary export restraints might also be subjected to a similar analysis, but these have been phased out under the WTO Agreements on Safeguards discussed above.

It is also worth noting that the standing requirements for initiating a dumping investigation, pursuant to the GATT-WTO framework may be viewed as more demanding for a complainant than is the case in competition proceedings. For a dumping case to proceed, there must be evidence that the complaint is made by domestic producers constituting more than 50% of the domestic production of the like product. This high standing requirement may act as a bar to frivolous or anti-competitive litigation. It might be worth considering whether, and under what circumstances, this standing requirement might facilitate collusive behaviour by competitors. Standing requirements under competition laws are not so stringent. However, in order to be allowed to petition competition authorities or to sue in courts, the parties need usually to demonstrate, in one way or the other, that they are potentially harmed by the alleged anti-competitive practices.

Similarly, antidumping and countervailing duty investigations are now subject to strict negotiated time limits codified in WTO Agreements. On the other hand, there is no such multilateral agreement and few domestic law requirements that limit the decision-making time in competition cases.

In some countries' views, the differences discussed above may not necessarily reflect inconsistencies between trade and competition policies which are (as is noted in the paper on "Complementarities between trade and competition policies") "in general complementary and mutually reinforcing." Rather, one needs to take into account the particular aims and specific legal, economic and institutional settings in which the two policies are applied. That being said, in some other countries' views, the differences discussed above show inconsistencies between trade and competition policies.

## Intellectual property

Intellectual property provides a very interesting example of the relationship between competition and trade policies. In part, the reason for this is rooted in the discussion of the efficiency objectives of both policies discussed in Section II of this paper, which discussed the relationship among productive, allocative and dynamic efficiency.

If government intervention hinders the development of new technologies, processes or products, over time the cumulative consequences for welfare will outweigh even large one-off changes in static allocative or productive efficiency. In addition to the effects on efficiency, innovation is an important source of new competition, both in adding new features and qualities to existing products and services and in the creation of completely new products and services which can supplant existing suppliers. For these reasons, competition authorities now place great value on innovation. There is, however, still a considerable debate about the best way to facilitate innovation which is at the heart of both trade and competition concerns with regard to intellectual property. Some commentators argue that protection of intellectual property rights spur innovation by ensuring compensation for an investor's investment, while allowing the diffusion of ideas that facilitates further innovation. This diffusion occurs in part from the fact that patent applications must be filed before there is protection. While intellectual property rights should thus promote the creation and diffusion of primary innovation, some argue that it may slow or deter secondary innovation. However, others argue that overly-broad intellectual property rights can actually slow or deter innovation by reducing the rate of diffusion of ideas or by reducing the incentives for an innovator to continue to develop new ideas due to the lack of active competition acting as an incentive for his or her behaviour.[8] These problems are counter-balanced by the following factors: (1) a patent must disclose inventions clearly enough to allow others to practice it; (2) most countries have research exceptions to patent rights; and (3) a profitable investment may induce others to "invent around" the patent, potentially leading to more competition.

Thus, while competition authorities apply the same standards and analytical methods to intellectual property as to other forms of property, the importance of preserving or encouraging dynamic efficiency may affect the result in particular cases. For this reason when competition policy is concerned with dynamic efficiency, as is often the case with intellectual property protectionist, it is careful to weigh as accurately as possible those efficiencies against possible anti-competitive effects. The 1995 US Department of Justice and Federal Trade Commission Antitrust Guidelines for the Licensing of Intellectual Property and the 1996 EU Technology Transfer Block Exemption set forth certain helpful principles for analysing how competition policy applies to intellectual property.

The WTO addressed intellectual property concerns in its Agreement on Trade-Related Aspects of Intellectual Property Rights ("TRIPs"). Like competition law, the TRIPs Agreement generally respects intellectual property rights subject to the rules and practices set forth in previous international agreements and conventions relating to intellectual property, and sets forth the minimum standards of enforcement to be applied in domestic law. Like competition law, the TRIPs Agreement is also concerned with the control of anti-competitive practices in contractual licenses. For example, Article 8 provides for each country to take appropriate measures in order to prevent the abuse of intellectual property rights. Articles 31 and 32 also address the abuse of intellectual property rights by providing rules for the application of competition law (measures taken by a competition authority and a judicial judgement). Article 40(2) provides that nothing in the TRIPs Agreement shall prevent Members from specifying in their legislation licensing practices or conditions that may in particular cases constitute an abuse of intellectual property rights having an adverse effect on competition in the relevant market. Moreover, a Member may adopt appropriate measures to prevent or control such practices, which may include, for example, exclusive grantback conditions, conditions preventing challenges to validity and coercive package licensing, in the light of the relevant laws and regulations of that Member. In this regard, it is at least arguable that the TRIPs Agreement functions, at least in part, by allowing for the enforcement of domestic competition policy. In this way, trade and competition policy are mutually reinforcing.

Article 6 of the TRIPs Agreement provides that nothing in the agreement shall be used to address the issue of the exhaustion of intellectual property rights. The issue of exhaustion is concerned with whether parallel imports should be prohibited or not. That being said, it may also be the case that trade law may permit trade in copyrighted or trademarked gray market goods in the name of both allocative and productive efficiency, while competition policy and intellectual property law (working from a dynamic efficiency objective) might not do so in all jurisdictions.[9]

Trade and competition policies may also share similar objectives with respect to standard setting. It may be the case that innovation or adoption of a particular technology is dependent on some general understanding or industry consensus about standards; e.g. access or interconnection. In these cases, both policies are also concerned with the potential for abuse. The WTO Agreement on Technical Barriers to Trade seeks to address this concern through a broad ex ante approach that puts the onus on governments to ensure that "national treatment" is applied by both governmental and non-governmental bodies. On the other hand, competition law tends to police the abuse of professional standard setting through *ad hoc* case by case enforcement. That being said, to the extent that individual prosecutions and sanctions alter the incentives for parties to engage in discriminatory standard setting practices, then competition policy might also have an *ex ante* effect. Thus while the two approaches may use different means to achieve their similar objectives, those differences need not give rise to any inconsistency of application, and in fact, might reinforce each other.

# NOTES

1.  Concern for productive efficiency gains in competition policy might lead in some circumstances in some jurisdictions to mergers that reduce costs to competitors being approved notwithstanding the short term reduction in consumer welfare arising from price increases.

2.  It may be that "hard core" export cartels are more likely to be to the detriment of foreign consumers than some other forms of export co-operation agreements that simply enable small exporters to compete effectively in a foreign market thus providing important price competition in the foreign market.

3.  When exporting countries have trade barriers that block re-importation of exported goods, antidumping laws may be seen as sharing similar objectives with competition laws that deal with price discrimination. In such cases, it may be possible to address the market segmentation concern by dealing with the trade barrier directly, rather than with price discrimination laws.

4.  In some countries, e.g. the United States, competition law distinguishes between "primary line", "secondary line" and "tertiary line" injury. Primary line injury concerns injury to competitors of the firm while secondary line injury concerns injury to downstream firms disadvantaged vis-a-vis other downstream firms. Tertiary line injury concerns injury to customers of the disfavoured buyers.

5.  However, it may be observed that there is no requirement or element of predation explicitly or implicitly in the GATT/WTO Agreements, nor does there appear to be a predatory pricing requirement in the implementing legislation of Members' trade remedy laws.

6.  Some jurisdictions such as the EU and Canada have gone further, and adopted a "lesser duty rule". The EU has included in its antidumping legislation a rule which provides that the EU applies the lower of the price in the country of export minus the price of the exported good in the Community and the price in the country of export minus the "constructed value" of the exported good in the Community. Canada has recently proposed amendments to its antidumping law that would permit the Canadian

International Trade Tribunal (the body which makes the determination of material injury to a domestic industry) to recommend to the Minister of Finance a reduced duty which would still be adequate to eliminate injury or the threat of injury as well as hinder the establishment or growth of an industry.

7. But it is worth noting that not all trade remedies are "offsetting". Some are indirectly offsetting and others are more akin to injunctive relief.

8. United States Federal Trade Commission, *Anticipating the 21st Century: Competition Policy in the New High-Tech, Global Marketplace, Volume I,* Chapter 6 (May 1996).

9. See Joan Biskupic, "Court Lets Discounters Keep Selling US-Made Goods They Buy Overseas" *Washington Post A7* (March 10, 1998).

*Chapter 3*

## COMPETITION AND TRADE EFFECTS OF VERTICAL RESTRAINTS

### Introduction

Vertical relationships range from transactions between completely independent enterprises to the integration of two or more levels within a single enterprise. Between these two extremes fall contractual arrangements which restrict the freedom of action of one or both of the upstream (generally speaking, a manufacturer) or downstream firm (usually a distributor). Vertical restraints include both price (e.g. minimum or maximum resale price maintenance - RPM) and non-price restraints (e.g. exclusive territorial or customer arrangements, service/support provisions, exclusive dealing, tie-ins, selective distribution, quantity forcing, and two-part tariffs or aggregated rebate schemes). Since such "vertical restraints" could potentially have a significant impact on trade, our joint work involved an examination of the theory and practice of such restraints, including how they are generally treated under competition law.

Joint work on vertical restraints began with a roundtable focused on exclusive dealing and exclusive territories agreements. Based on the results of that roundtable, a statement on vertical relationships and market access was included in the 1994 Ministerial report. Another roundtable discussion was held, this time centred on automobile and auto parts distribution. The Joint Group then embarked on examining a series of real and hypothetical cases:

    a) February 1997 - the first hypothetical exclusive dealing case presented by the US delegation (First US Hypothetical).

    b) February 1997 - whitegood sales in New Zealand presented by the Australian and New Zealand delegations (New Zealand Whitegoods).

c) June 1997 - exclusive dealing in marmalade presented by the Secretariat (Marmalade I).

d) October 1997 - a return to exclusive dealing in marmalade (Marmalade II).

e) October 1997 - exclusive territories in silicon strips presented by the Secretariat (Silicon Strips).

f) June 1998 - vertical restraints hypothetical case presented by the US delegation (Second US Hypothetical).

This chapter advances the joint work by drawing together some conclusions that both trade and competition officials can support. It does this in the next two sections: Section I presents the highlights of what was contained in the synthesis of past CLP Committee work on vertical restraints, a synthesis already considered by the Joint Group, while Section II, based on the three pertinent Secretariat notes plus Aides-mémoires of the various case discussions, proposes areas of possible consensus in the work so far. Section III suggests that areas remain for further discussion.

## I.      Highlights from synthesis of past CLP Committee work

The analysis presented below is simplified by focusing on goods for resale, where upstream firms produce "brands" and distributors provide services in reselling these. The producers are referred to as the "upstream" part of the industry and the distributors as the "downstream". Despite this simplification, it should be apparent that the general arguments carry over to concerns about intermediate production, where the input supplied by an upstream firm is transformed by a downstream producer, as well as situations where producers are subjected to restraints agreed with distributors.

It is long standing practice in many jurisdictions to distinguish price restraints, i.e. RPM, from non-price vertical restraints. Minimum RPM is widely prohibited *per se* (except in certain areas, such as books), i.e. treated as illegal regardless of claimed competitive effects. In contrast, maximum RPM and non-price vertical restraints are increasingly subject to a rule of reason, i.e. case by case analysis of pro-competitive and anti-competitive effects. All but one of the examples referred to below concern non-price restraints, and it must be noted at the outset that what is said about market structure and other indicia of market power are not reached where a particular restraint is prohibited *per se* or where price or non-price restraints are employed as part of a collusive scheme to restrict competition.

The economic effects of vertical restraints can be grouped into two general categories: effects on vertical co-ordination and on market competition. The former is concerned with the benefits which may result from solving problems which might otherwise arise in distribution and supply and detract from aggregate profits. The latter category refers to effects that vertical restraints may have on competition in the market. As will be argued below, one or a set of vertical restraints could have both pro-competitive and anti-competitive effects so that the net effect on competition and on economic efficiency is not obvious *a priori*. Pro-competitive effects could basically arise through improved co-ordination among different levels of the vertical chain leading from raw materials and component parts to finished goods and on through distribution channels to final consumers. Anti-competitive effects could possibly result if vertical restraints either facilitate collusion or exclude/foreclose actual or potential competitors.

## *Vertical co-ordination and some effects on competition and efficiency*

Where the supply of goods or services proceeds through successive vertical levels, the complementary nature of such vertical linkages means that co-ordination between them takes on considerable importance. The decisions of this structure, some taken by the upstream firm and some by the downstream firm, determine the nature and quality of the product or service supplied, its cost, and the price and locations at which it is sold; in other words, these decisions determine the economic efficiency with which the product or service is supplied. The terms of an agreement organise the vertical relationship and help co-ordinate what otherwise would be independent, sub-optimal (in terms of total profitability of the firms concerned) decisions.

Three categories of co-ordinating provisions or vertical restraints can be distinguished. First, the parties could agree to give the producer direct control over distribution decisions (for example, give producers the right to specify retail services or prices), or equivalently give the distributor control over supply decisions (e.g. grant distributors the right to specify the inputs and methods used by the producer). Second, vertical restraints could restructure incentives. For example, through using a two-part tariff combining a lump sum fee plus a per unit price set at marginal cost, producers could make distributors feel the full effects of their decisions on aggregate profits. Third, where there are spillover effects among distributors, vertical restraints could reduce or eliminate intrabrand competition, thereby reducing or eliminating "free-riding".

For example, consider the situation where distributors are unwilling to supply important in-store information because customers can obtain the information then avoid paying for it by simply crossing the street and buying the same goods at a discounter. This problem can be greatly mitigated by assigning large exclusive territories to each distributor.[1] There can also be free-riding among producers as where one producer engages in extensive informative advertising and other producers choose instead to offer lower prices to distributors. When consumers enter a store to buy the advertised good, the storeowner will have an incentive to steer the purchaser to the lower priced competing product (on which he earns a higher profit margin). That kind of free-riding can be eliminated through the use of exclusive dealing (i.e. requiring distributors to carry only a single producer's goods). While exclusive dealing will reduce in-store interbrand competition, it could well improve overall interbrand competition and increase consumer surplus (i.e. the difference between the maximum that consumers would pay for the current quantity consumed and the amount they are actually paying).

In addition to situations where vertical restraints reduce intrabrand competition or in-store interbrand competition but may nevertheless increase overall competition and efficiency, there could be circumstances where such restraints help to reduce problems associated with market power. In particular, where both producers and distributors have market power and are earning supra-competitive profits, distributors left to their own devices will only consider the effects on their own profits when deciding whether or not to raise their prices. They would totally ignore the fact that from the perspective of producers, distributor price increases simply reduce the amount sold with no compensating increase in the price received by a producer. As a result, when such distributors increase their prices, not only is consumer surplus reduced, combined manufacturer and distributor profits might fall as well. In this "double margin" situation, manufacturers, distributors and consumers could all potentially be better off if distributors lost their power to set prices.[2]

While not denying the potential for vertical restraints to improve consumer welfare, it is also true that the choice of product quality or distribution service that maximises total manufacturer and distributor profits will not necessarily be the choice that maximises economic efficiency, i.e. combined consumer and producer surplus (where producer surplus equals profits above and beyond a normal return on investment). For example, provisions that allow profitable price discrimination may or may not increase efficiency. The greater the competition that the vertical system faces from other suppliers, however, the more its members will be collectively constrained to make choices that increase economic efficiency.

The extent of competition from other brands and distributors may though be reduced through the use of vertical arrangements. For example, minimum RPM may help to sustain high prices by making it easier for producers to monitor cheating on a collusive agreement, which in turn increases the incentives to create cartels. Moreover, minimum RPM could be used to support a distributors' cartel, whereby the producer is used as the instrument to set and then monitor a collusive price level. The same could be said of exclusive territories compelled by powerful distributors especially in situations where such restraints are not manifestly necessary to protect distributors' brand specific investments.

It is also possible to strategically use vertical restrictions to dampen competition. For example, if exclusive dealing is widely practised, consumers are required to visit other stores to find competing products and compare their attributes and prices, something consumers may be reluctant to do for low valued items or those required urgently or purchased on impulse. Higher customer search costs could thereby translate into higher average prices and lower consumer surplus. Furthermore, restrictions that decrease intrabrand competition among distributors, e.g. by assigning exclusive territories, may also decrease competition at the upstream level by making producers' price cuts less attractive. That result flows from the fact that reduced competition among distributors means less pressure to pass any producer price cuts on to consumers. If price cuts might simply end up fattening distributor profits, producers will have less incentive to make such cuts.

Vertical restraints also may reduce competition in the long run if they can be used to erect significant barriers to entry and if competition is not already substantial. In regard to competition at the producer level, most attention has focused on the role of long-term exclusive dealing arrangements (and provisions which can provide the same effects, e.g. full-line forcing and aggregated rebate schemes) in raising barriers to entry which may have the effect of excluding or foreclosing foreign or domestic competitors. Such arrangements between a producer and its distributors prevent other producers from distributing their brands through these agents. When exclusive dealing or other vertical restraints having similar effects are adopted by a dominant firm or are used by a sufficiently large number of producers, they can effectively raise rivals' costs by requiring them to use alternative less efficient marketing channels. The increased distribution costs may then be sufficiently high to deter entry.

On the other hand, it is conceivable that vertical restraints can promote entry and competition. When restraints increase profits without raising entry barriers, either through increased efficiency or increased oligopolist co-ordination, they promote entry. In addition, if restraints increase the returns that can be earned from investments in know-how, they promote investment in know-how, which in turn may lead to entry and both new brands and new distributors.

The dynamic effects of vertical restraints on markets take on particular significance from a trade perspective where a restraint such as exclusive dealing may impede or alternatively facilitate market access. For instance, new entry by a foreign firm may be considerably more difficult if non-price vertical restraints tie up existing domestic distribution systems, especially if these are reinforced by laws and regulations or other barriers to entry inhibiting foreign firms from setting up alternative distribution channels. This difficulty is increased if the restraints will run for many years but would be decreased if the market is expanding or alternative distribution systems are being created. On the other hand, new entry might be facilitated by vertical restraints if a new entrant needs to offer an exclusive arrangement to induce a distributor to efficiently promote a new product. Accordingly, the effects of vertical restraints on trade are likely to depend on, amongst other things, the type of restraint, the collective market share of firms practising the restraint, the nature of the market, the duration of the restraint, and whether restraint renewal/expiration dates are staggered or grouped together.

## General lessons from economic analysis

We have seen that vertical restraints are likely to arise in many different circumstances and could have a variety of effects on competition and economic efficiency. Because these effects depend heavily on the facts and may vary over time, it is difficult to recommend *a priori* that a given vertical restraint should be considered to be either legal or illegal in all situations. *Rather a case-by-case, "rule of reason" approach, one that seeks to balance "pro" and anti-competitive effects, is very much called for.* Moreover, economic analysis provides several other insights of relevance to both competition and trade policy makers.

> 1. *The extent of interbrand competition (including its in-store component) as well as intrabrand competition are crucial factors in the analysis of the effects of vertical restraints.*

Where the vertical structure faces strong competition both from other brands and from other distributors, there is little potential for any type of vertical restraint to reduce economic efficiency.[3]

48

2. *Where general market conditions leave open the question of whether a vertical restraint will increase or reduce efficiency, economic analysis provides guidance for identifying those specific circumstances in which a particular restraint may impact on competition or efficiency.*

For example, it identifies circumstances in which exclusive dealing by either a dominant firm or which is widespread in the market might be used to diminish competition by raising entry barriers, and other circumstances in which reduced in-store interbrand competition might increase over-all interbrand competition by preventing free-riding. Specifically, reduced competition may be expected to result when competition is already limited at both the producer and distributor level and restraints significantly raise rivals' costs. On the other hand, increased competition may be predicted from exclusive dealing required to justify efficient manufacturer advertising which would otherwise be undermined by producer free-riding. More generally, free-riding aspects appear more problematic (and thus provide a stronger efficiency argument) for goods which are complex, technical, expensive, one-off purchases and distributed through non-convenience outlets. This is especially so if consumers have limited product knowledge and have difficulty assessing the product's attributes prior to purchase and consumption, conditions more likely to hold for new rather than established products.

3. *It is the degree of competition prevailing in a market that is the key factor in determining the effects of vertical restraints on economic efficiency.*

Analysis should cover the extent of competition in the market from other competing brands and from other distribution systems, rather than being centred on intrabrand competition. Vertical restraints may reduce intrabrand competition without harming economic efficiency. With sufficient competition from other brands and distributors, a producer will be unable to reduce economic efficiency by exercising market power over pricing or the choice of quality in a properly defined market even if intrabrand competition is completely eliminated. However, when interbrand competition is limited, then restrictions on intrabrand competition may take on some importance as they may serve to dampen further interbrand competition.

4. *A properly drawn antitrust market must group together what consumers regard as all good substitutes (in both the product and geographic senses).*

A lack of competition in butter sales in Country X has little significance if a significant, non-transitory price increase in butter prices in Country X would simply cause consumers to substitute margarine or to begin to source butter and margarine supplies from producers located outside the country.

> 5.  *As a short hand measure of probable degree of competition, law enforcers should consider market structure in determining when a vertical restraint is acceptable.*

Vertical restraints are very unlikely to harm economic efficiency or reduce competition in a properly defined market with low concentration, negligible barriers to entry, and a rapid rate of technological change.

> 6.  *The analysis should consider both long-run (dynamic) and short-run (static) effects of vertical restraints.*

Even if a vertical restraint has a negative or ambiguous effect in the short run, its net long-run effect may be positive because the restraint leads to increased entry or investment in intellectual property. Alternatively, its long run effect may be detrimental if new entry or capacity is inhibited such that competition and incentives to innovate are both reduced.

> 7.  *The analysis should consider what is the most likely alternative to a vertical restraint, e.g. operating without the restraint, employing an alternative one, cease trading, or vertically integrating.*

Vertical restraints are one means of integrating decision-making. If a particular restraint is not available, the alternative may be not less integration but a different method of vertical integration, e.g. common ownership, which may be neither more efficient nor more likely to promote interbrand or intrabrand competition, although it is conceivable that closer vertical links involving more mutual agreements may be more desirable than vertical restraints.

In addition to the points listed above, it is clear that policy design needs to consider enforcement costs. One way to reduce the enforcement costs of case-by-case analysis is to develop enforcement guidelines, as a number of competition policy authorities already have. Guidelines can increase the predictability of reviews thus generally enhancing compliance as well as reduce the number of cases requiring detailed analysis by including criteria and procedures for identifying those cases where there is a risk of anti-competitive effect and where more detailed analysis may be necessary.

Enforcement costs may be further reduced by establishing different rules or enforcement guidelines depending on the state of competition in the market. In this regard it may be appropriate to adopt the following general approaches:

- Firms with small market shares in unconcentrated upstream and downstream markets, and new or established firms attempting to enter a new market could have presumptive permission to include vertical restrictions; only the minimal analysis needed to establish competitive market conditions is necessary to determine the economic effects.

- Vertical systems that are widespread in their market could face a more detailed inquiry into the extent of competition in their market and, if necessary, into the effects of the proposed vertical restraints.

- Vertical systems practised by a dominant firm could require a more detailed justification to show that the restraints do not pose substantial risks to product competition, would enhance efficiency, and that comparable benefits cannot be realised with lower risks for product competition.

## II.    Shared conclusions

In the course of considering the review of previous CLP Committee work on vertical restraints, studying the other two Secretariat papers, and discussing various case examples, trade and competition policy makers have come to agree on a great deal concerning the effects of vertical restraints on their respective domains. The following is an attempt to briefly list these points of agreement, including a few areas where the two communities have simply come to better appreciate the constraints under which the other works.

1. Vertical restraints have complex potential pro and anti-competitive effects. They can also enhance or reduce market access by foreign-based competitors. Accordingly, vertical restraints call for a careful case by case, "rule of reason" (i.e. balancing) analysis. In markets sufficiently populated by competing firms, vertical restraints cannot be presumed to be anti-competitive simply because they raise rivals' costs, though they should be subject to increased scrutiny the more they potentially exclude new foreign and domestic entrants.

2. The pro and anti-competitive effects of vertical restraints must be judged in the context of properly defined antitrust markets grouping together products and production locations which consumers consider to be good substitutes. The geographic dimension of such markets could extend beyond a single country, especially if barriers to international trade are low or non-existent.[4] An emphasis on substitutability is central to market definition for competition analysis because the ultimate purpose for making the definition is to provide a context for estimating the existence/extent of market power. There is no market power in situations where consumers could escape harm from anti-competitive pricing by easily substituting other products or geographic sources.[5]

3. With the exception of vertical restraints being used to facilitate collusion, it is highly improbable that such restraints will have net anti-competitive effects unless there is either: (a) market power on at least one level of a properly defined market; or (b) the restraint, either on its own or in concert with other vertical restraints, has the power to exclude or disadvantage a significant number of competitors (or a uniquely significant competitor or class of competitors) by virtue of its being widely used in the negatively affected market(s). The usual first step in gauging market power is to estimate whether incumbent market shares are high enough to permit unilateral anti-competitive pricing, or to facilitate collusion. Where that is in fact the case, the analysis normally proceeds to examine barriers to entry, i.e. considers whether there is reason to believe that anti-competitive pricing will be unprofitable because it will quickly encourage existing or new firms to increase supply to the market.

4. Where it is necessary to take a close look at barriers to entry, both competition and trade officials will be especially interested in whether governmental action (or inaction) are contributing to such barriers. Generally speaking, governmentally created or reinforced barriers to entry are among the most durable, hence serious constraints on competition. It follows that the existence of such barriers to entry could greatly increase the chances that competition officials will conclude that significant market power exists and action is warranted against vertical restraints affecting a particular market. Competition and trade officials should work together to reduce unwarranted governmental restrictions on competition and market access.[6] They should also of course co-operate to reduce all

types of anti-competitive private restraints that reduce market access.

5.  The primary objective of competition agencies is to promote economic efficiency by enhancing or protecting the competitive process rather than individual competitors. It follows that competition agencies will not necessarily be willing or able to take action against a vertical restraint merely because it harms certain actual or potential competitors, whatever their nationality might happen to be. In addition, extensive market analysis may be called for to assess anti-competitive effects.[7] At the same time, competition laws applied to promote economic efficiency can, in appropriate cases, also promote market access by for example, simultaneously addressing any anti-competitive exclusion or foreclosure of foreign firms or products.[8]

6.  The primary objectives of trade agencies in cases involving vertical restraints are to determine whether the restraints impede market access, and if so, to encourage or require the concerned government(s) to remedy the situation. Compared with competition agencies, trade officials will attach greater significance to: (a) governmental action that affects the power of vertical restraints to exclude or disadvantage competitors; (b) possible discriminatory or differential effects of vertical restraints on foreign versus domestic competitors; (c) the potential for foreign firms to provide a qualitatively different kind of competition than might be available from domestic firms; and (d) the potential for competition policy analysis to underestimate the potential gains from trade in evaluating whether to intervene in a given vertical restraint case, thus erring on the side of inaction. Trade officials generally have more power than competition agencies to press for a change in government policy in cases where such policy undergirds a vertical restraint restricting market access or otherwise hindering competition between foreign and domestic firms. This is especially true where the impugned vertical restraint may not have anti-competitive effects under the analysis typically employed by OECD competition agencies. In these circumstances, competition and trade officials should work together to reduce these unwarranted governmental restrictions on competition and market access, bearing in mind that some such restrictions might be fully compatible with WTO obligations.

7. Both anti-competitive effect and negative impact on access by foreign producers are more likely to be associated with vertical restraints the longer their terms. The pro-competitive effects could also be stronger the longer the vertical restraints' terms. Claims that some vertical restraints have pro-competitive efficiency effects and a potential to either assist or restrict market access are more likely to be credible and significant the more technically sophisticated, expensive and infrequently purchased is a product.

8. Competition agencies should continue to improve information sharing and enforcement assistance co-operation so as to more effectively address vertical restraint cases which cross borders.

## III.     Further reflection

The above points represent a significant body of shared learning which has been fostered by the Joint Group and its predecessor Joint Working Party. Though much has been accomplished, there remain some important questions meriting continued exploration.[9, 10, 11]

# NOTES

1. Setting <u>minimum</u> permitted resale prices, i.e. (minimum) RPM, where legally permitted is another way of doing the same thing.

2. This could justify, in appropriate cases, the use of (maximum) RPM whereby a manufacturer sets the maximum resale price a distributor can charge. Essentially the same result could be obtained by requiring distributors to achieve and sustain minimum unit sales levels.

3. The reader is reminded that virtually all OECD countries make a distinction between price and non-price vertical restraints, and treat at least minimum RPM as illegal *per se*. Under such laws, the extents of interbrand and intrabrand competition have no significance so would not need to be determined in pertinent cases.

4. There is nothing contradictory about a competition agency stating that it is empowered to protect only domestic interests, yet recognising that the market for a particular good is international in size. Consumers could be just as well protected by the prospect that higher domestic prices would attract increased imports as by the possibility that higher prices would cause domestic producers to increase their outputs.

5. Marmalade I and II provided ample scope to explore market definition, and to note its importance in competition and trade cases.

6. Discussion of the Marmalade I and Silicon Strips cases illustrated competition and trade officials' concerns about how government regulations might affect the anti-competitive potential of vertical restraints. Another area that has several times been discussed in joint meetings is the question of parallel imports. Under current laws, copyright holders are able to licence their intellectual property in a way which segments national markets, reduces trade, and preserves international price discrimination that could potentially be anti-competitive.

7. The New Zealand Whitegoods case provided a good illustration of these important points. New Zealand competition law requires much more than merely showing that Australian whitegoods manufacturers found it difficult to enter the New Zealand market because of exclusive dealing practised by a

domestic producer accounting for some 80% of sales in New Zealand. To obtain relief under New Zealand competition law, the Australian firms would have had to demonstrate that the New Zealand firm benefiting from exclusive dealing had a dominant position in a properly drawn antitrust market and that it was using its market power in an unreasonable way. Establishing either of those points would require probing actual market conditions and would be a very fact intensive exercise.

8.        For example, in the case of the First U.S. Hypothetical, at least one Member's competition law might have found that the manufacturers enjoyed collective dominance and could have been prohibited from using threats of refusal to deal plus practices of progressive rebates to maintain an exclusive dealing system that appeared to inhibit market access.

9.        Consider for example a case where Country A's competition authority concerns itself solely with national or domestic welfare (the normal case), and also evaluates vertical restraints under a total economic surplus instead of the more common consumer surplus standard. Suppose there is a particular exclusive dealing restraint which happens to raise prices in Country A, hence reduces consumer surplus in that country. Suppose further that the exclusive dealing also increases producer/distributor surplus by more than enough to offset the reduction in consumer surplus. The exclusive dealing might therefore be permitted, but only if enough of the increase in the producer/distributor profits accrues to enterprises owned by the country's nationals because increased profits accruing to foreign owners would not be counted as offsetting harm to Country A's consumers. A variant of this example would be a situation where competition officials are willing to include producer/distribution surplus in the balance provided the producers/distributors are located in their jurisdiction (i.e. the competition authority applies a domestic welfare standard). In that case there is a potential for discrimination according to location rather than ownership of the firms involved.

10.      To illustrate one possibility, let us turn to another hypothetical exclusive dealing example. Suppose that such restraints in a particular market are very widespread in Country A, but older established, mostly domestically owned/based producers have no particular problems distributing their goods. In addition, let us assume that the incumbent producers have satisfied Country A's competition officials that the exclusive dealing arrangements benefit consumers through enhanced interbrand competition based on improved manufacturer supplied information, and in any case, there is no evidence that incumbents are either inefficient or earning supra-competitive profits.

Despite all the preceding assumed "facts", suppose producers in Country B establish that all that stops them from selling to Country A consumers are the exclusive dealing practices of existing sellers. In particular they demonstrate that:

a)  barriers to entry into distribution prevent them from setting up new parallel distribution systems in Country A;

b)  they offer a product significantly different (but still within the same antitrust market) from what is currently on offer in Country A; and

c)  they are profitably selling their products in other countries having the same product array they would have to compete against in Country A, but lacking the exclusive dealing arrangements found in Country A's market.

Faced with the above situation, Country B's trade policy officials might understandably try to persuade Country A's competition officials to prohibit the market access inhibiting exclusive dealing arrangements. They might also receive help from Country B's competition officials assuming they are mandated to advance Country B's producers' interests. Despite such interventions, Country A's competition officials would naturally be reluctant to prohibit exclusive dealing which they believe benefits Country A's consumers. Moreover, they would likely be quick to point out that they would be just as reluctant to help any Country A producers who might similarly complain about their inability to sell to Country A consumers.

It is worth noting that the above example has some similarity to the Second US Hypothetical presented by the US delegation to the Joint Group's 7th meeting.

11.  The Second US Hypothetical begins by noting that:

> In some cases, foreign goods embody different perspectives on production methods, different product design and development ideas, and other physical or non-physical factors that are either unknown or unavailable in the importing country. Exposing domestic firms to these factors can lead to product and technological advancement that would not be possible with domestic perspectives and ideas alone.

The hypothetical concedes that such gains from trade cannot always easily be estimated at the time an initial decision must be made concerning whether or not to permit one or a series of vertical restraints. It explores what trade and competition officials could and should do if a set of vertical restraints which, focusing solely on existing domestic products, offers a net improvement in consumer welfare despite an associated severe foreclosure effect. Two possible situations are proposed. Under the first, nothing is known about potential foreign competition at the time the vertical restraints are being considered for approval. Under the second, foreign potential entrants oppose permitting the restraints. In the context of the initial assumption that foreign enterprises may be able to offer especially valuable competition, the hypothetical seeks to explore whether or not competition agencies should make a special effort to assess the effects of foreclosure on foreign firms, and what informational hurdles would have to be surmounted to make that possible. The hypothetical urges greater co-operation among trade and competition agencies both within and across countries.

*Chapter 4*

# COMPETITION ELEMENTS IN INTERNATIONAL TRADE AGREEMENTS: A POST-URUGUAY ROUND OVERVIEW OF WTO AGREEMENTS

## Introduction

This overview attempts to avoid adopting any predetermined perspective vis-à-vis the desirability of any particular approach to the trade and competition interface. It has the more limited aim of examining, in a preliminary way, what World Trade Organization (WTO) Agreements may be considered to cover by way of competition-related matters. In doing so, however, it attempts to take an "open-minded" view on how far those agreements may actually go, with a view to stimulating further reflection and discussion. It does not deal with bilateral agreements on enforcement co-operation, or United Nations Conference on Trade and Development (UNCTAD) provisions on restrictive business practices, since the focus here is the trade-competition interface. Nor does it deal with other trade agreements with a more regional focus - e.g. North American Free Trade Agreement (NAFTA), Australia-New-Zealand Closer Economic Relations Trade Agreement (ANZCERTA), etc. - as this would have meant a significantly longer paper. It remains possible, of course, to extend the analysis to the latter if there was a wish to do so in light of the priorities for future work.

## I.     General overview

There is a complex overlap between competition concepts and norms and those of trade liberalisation:[1]

In some instances, the removal of border trade barriers may provide only limited market access in the absence of action on, for example, monopoly or market dominance issues. Such matters - from a domestic policy perspective - may be the prime subject matter of competition policy. This is the case in a number of services sectors, of which telecommunications is perhaps the clearest example.

In other cases (where significant liberalisation has already occurred through removal of tariffs and other border measures) there is potential for restrictive practices of various kinds to undermine the value of concessions. For instance, the way technical standards are developed (e.g. by industry associations or private standards-writing bodies), promulgated, and translated into mandatory measures may lead to restriction of market access. Similar issues arise where self-regulating professions or associations control entry through licensing and certification. Along the same lines, public and private monopoly may become instruments of protection of a particularly non-transparent kind, favouring local providers for example in their purchasing decisions (hence, the General Agreement on Tariffs and Trade (GATT) provisions on State Trading Enterprises and the panel litigation surrounding, e.g. the practices of Canadian provincial liquor boards).

Thirdly, it has been argued that some issues that have traditionally been conceptualised as *trade* matters may be usefully reconceived when approached from the perspective of being competition problems that could be addressed through either the application of competition concepts within trade institutions, or transboundary application of domestic competition law (the oft-cited example being anti-dumping).

Fourth, trade agreements may need to hedge the possibility of certain kinds of market access guarantees being misused for anti-competitive purposes.

## II.     The World Trade Organization Agreements (WTO)

### *The General Agreement on Tariff & Trade (GATT)*

While the provisions of GATT have been interpreted as dealing primarily with trade-restricting practices of governments, a number of GATT provisions appear to bear, directly or indirectly, on business practices. This note outlines some of the potentially relevant provisions.

*Article II:4*

Paragraph II:4 provides:

> "If any contracting party establishes, maintains or authorises, formally or in effect, a monopoly of the importation of any product described in the appropriate Schedule annexed to this Agreement, such monopoly shall not, except as provided for in that Schedule or as otherwise agreed between the parties which initially negotiated the concession, operate so as to afford protection on the average in excess of the amount of protection provided for in that Schedule."

This provision is based on a recognition that there are "behind the border" practices that can raise the level of protection against imports beyond that which is provided for by border measures bound in a Member's Schedule. It would appear to aim at disciplining those practices so that commitments on border protection are not effectively circumvented. In this case, there is a proscription of conduct by an import monopoly that operates to afford protection "on the average" in excess of that provided for by the bound level of protection for the product in question. This applies where a contracting party "establishes, maintains or authorises" the import monopoly "formally or in effect".

When it comes to interpreting the kinds of practices covered by this provision, it may be useful to recall the reasoning followed by the 1988 Panel under GATT (1947) with respect to the Canadian import, distribution and sale of alcoholic drinks by provincial marketing authorities.[2]

The Panel found that, in this case, differential mark-ups on imported as opposed to domestic alcoholic beverages could only be justified to the extent that such a differential was commensurate with differential costs of marketing the imported products. In arriving at this conclusion, the Panel was required to address argumentation that the differential was nonetheless warranted on grounds of "normal commercial considerations". In doing so, the Panel addressed matters such as what would constitute the normal commercial behaviour of firms, and normal conditions of competition:

> "The Panel noted Canada's statement that, in some instances, the differential mark-ups also reflected a policy of revenue maximisation on the part of provincial liquor boards, which charged higher mark-ups on imported than on domestic alcoholic beverages because they marketed imported products as premium products and exploited less-

price elastic demand for these products, and that this policy was in accordance with the General Agreement because revenue maximisation was justified by normal commercial considerations.

The panel considered that a monopoly profit margin on imports resulting from policies of revenue maximisation by provincial liquor boards could not normally be considered as a "reasonable margin of profit".....[I]n accordance with the normal meaning of these words in their context of Article II and Article 31 of the Havana Charter...." *a reasonable margin of profit" was a margin of profit that would be obtained under normal conditions of competition (in the absence of the monopoly)."*

This provision has particular interest because it rests on a clear recognition that certain practices inside the border which are a function of market structure (in this case, exploitation of monopoly power) should be taken into account when it comes to assessing whether or not market access is being maintained and should be, accordingly, covered by "trade" obligations. It is the **overall** protective effect, inclusive of certain market structure factors, that is to be evaluated. The provision applies only to monopoly for the import of goods, not the distribution of goods.

However, if the fundamental object and purpose of this provision is to secure the integrity of market access commitments against impediments based on certain forms of internal market structure, how far does that extend? It seems clear that the provision covers monopolies, whether public or private, where those monopoly rights are granted by formal governmental measures, such as legislation or regulation, and it was certainly an instance of this kind that was covered by the Panel Report referred to above. Thus the provision appears to cover what might be called "direct" governmental measures where the monopoly is itself a public entity. It would also appear to cover the situation where the particular actions at issue may be undertaken by an entity that is itself "private" but the fact that it has been authorised as a monopoly in the first place is sufficient to bring it under the discipline.

Furthermore, the adverbial wording *"in effect"* suggests that the obligation may be applicable also in certain circumstances where there is not even formal authorisation by the government. Under this interpretation, the question may be raised as to whether the absence of formal government authorisation would not necessarily be sufficient to quarantine, e.g. certain exclusive distribution and retailing networks for imported products from coverage by this provision. On this basis, the obligation would be equally applicable in circumstances where, as a matter of fact, a monopoly is *effectively* established, authorised or maintained by the government.

It may also be noted in this context that the requirement that "protection" may not be increased above the bound level does not appear to be restricted to a particular class of conduct. It would appear to cover any conduct - whether explicitly targeted at imports or not - which impedes the competitive opportunity for imports. Thus, in the 1992 Panel Report on Canadian Import, Distribution and Sale of Certain Alcoholic Drinks by Provincial Marketing Agencies (*Beer*)[3] a Panel found that a minimum price requirement imposed by a government-sanctioned monopoly violated National Treatment, even though imposed on both domestic and foreign product, as it was set in such a way as to limit the ability of lower-cost foreign producers to compete on price.

It may be worth noting that in its 1989 Report on Korean Restrictions on Imports of Beef, the Panel took the view that the Interpretative Notes to the GATT required Article II:4 to be interpreted in accordance with Article 31 of the Havana Charter.[4] Article 31:5 provided that import monopolies would import and offer for sale such quantities of the product as will be sufficient to satisfy the full domestic demand for the imported product". The Panel considered it inappropriate to apply Article II:4 in view of the existence of quantitative restrictions in this case. It stressed, however, that "in the absence of quantitative restrictions, an import monopoly was not to afford protection, on the average, in excess of the amount of protection provided for in the relevant schedule, as set out in Article II:4."

*Article III*

Article III, relating to the national treatment obligation may well be of importance when it comes to competition related matters. This provision is fundamentally about the maintenance of competitive conditions, independent of actual trade effects. It may be useful to note certain aspects of Panel reasoning on this point. In the 1987 Panel Report on United States Taxes on Petroleum and Certain Imported Substances (Superfund),[5] it is noted:

> "Article III:2, first sentence, obliges contracting parties to establish certain competitive conditions for imported products in relation to domestic products. Unlike some other provisions in the General Agreement, it does not refer to trade effects... A demonstration that a measure inconsistent with Article III:2 first sentence, has no or insignificant effects would therefore in the view of the panel not be a

sufficient demonstration that the benefits accruing under that provision had not been nullified or impaired."

It may also be noted that more recently, the 1998 Panel Report on Japanese Measures Affecting Consumer Photographic Film and Paper also considered the meaning of "competitive conditions" in Article III:4.[6] The Panel stated that:

"We recall our earlier findings (with respect to the Article XXIII:1(b) non-violation complaints) that none of the eight distribution "measures" cited by the United States had been shown to discriminate against imported products, either in terms of a *de jure* discrimination (a measure that discriminates *on its face* as to the origin of products) or in terms of a *de facto* discrimination (a measure that in its application upsets the relative competitive position between domestic and imported products, as it existed at the time when a relevant tariff concession was granted). In this connection, it could be argued that the standard we enunciated and applied under Article XXIII:1(b) - that of "upsetting the competitive relationship" - may be different from the standard of "upsetting effective equality of competitive opportunities" applicable to Article III:4. However, we do not see any significant distinction between the two standards apart from the fact that this Article III:4 standard calls for no less favourable treatment for imported products in general, whereas the Article XXIII:1(b) standard calls for a comparison of the competitive relationship between foreign and domestic products at two specific points in time, i.e., when the concession was granted and currently.... Here, as in our examination of the same measures in light of the US claim of non-violation nullification or impairment, the evidence cited by the United States indicates that the measures neither (i) discriminate on their face against imported film or paper (they are formally neutral as to the origin of products), nor (ii) in their application have a disparate impact on imported film or paper..... Additionally, as we also noted earlier, single brand wholesale distribution is the common market structure - indeed the norm - in most major national film markets, including the US market. It is unclear why the same economic forces acting to promote single brand wholesale distribution in the United States would not also exist in Japan... Accordingly, and essentially for the reasons already stated in our findings on non-violation nullification and impairment, we find that the United States has failed to demonstrate that any of the distribution "measures" in issue accords less favourable treatment to imported film and paper than to film and paper of Japanese origin. The US claim under Article III:4 must therefore be rejected."[7]

As to the reach of this National Treatment obligations regarding imports, it applies "in respect of all laws, regulations and requirements *affecting* their internal sale, offering for sale, purchase, transportation, distribution or use." (emphasis added).

A number of questions may arise in this context. Is a competition law a "law, regulation or requirement" in the sense of Article III? If so, are there situations where those laws can "affect" internal sale, offering for sale, purchase, transportation, distribution or use of imports as well as domestic production? If so, would the obligations be potentially breached in any situation where, as a matter of fact, those laws favour domestically produced goods over imports?

This, it may be noted, is not a question of whether there is a national treatment obligation as regards the actual private practices themselves. Rather, it is a question of the manner in which the actual competition law or regulation itself is applied when it comes to matters that affect the competitive relationship of imported and domestically produced goods.

It may be worth noting in this context the reasoning that has been used by Panels when addressing disputes relating to the obligations of Article III. The cases concerned reflect a view that there is no reason to interpret the term "affecting" in a restrictive manner. For instance, the 1958 Panel on Italian Discrimination Against Imported Agricultural Machinery[8] noted that:

> "...the text of paragraph 4 referred .to laws and regulations and requirements *affecting* internal sale, purchase, etc., and not to laws, regulations and requirements governing the conditions of sale or purchase. The selection of the word "affecting" would imply...that the drafters of the article intended to cover in paragraph 4 not only the laws and regulations which directly governed the conditions of sale or purchase but also any laws or regulations which might adversely modify the conditions of competition between the domestic and imported products in the internal market." [emphasis in the original].

This reasoning was followed also by the more recent 1989 Panel Report on United States Section 337 of the Tariff Act of 1930.[9] That panel noted, *inter alia*, that:

"the text of Article III:4 makes no distinction between substantive and procedural laws, regulations and requirements enforcement procedures cannot be separated from the substantive provisions they serve to enforce... Nor could the applicability of Article III:4 be denied on the grounds that most of the procedures in the case before the Panel are applied to persons rather than products"

Bearing the above in mind, it may be worth considering, by way of illustration, the subject of the "rights of foreign firms" from this perspective. The conclusion of that survey appears to be that there is, in fact, no discrimination between "foreign" as opposed to "domestic" firms when it comes to respective rights in respect of competition proceedings. What if that had not been the case? One could take the example of the right to bring a private anti-trust suit. If it was the case that a "foreign" firm (which exported goods to the market concerned and considered that certain firm behaviour in the market concerned was impeding its exports) did not have access to such a right but domestic firms did, could this be considered to be a matter covered by Article III of the General Agreement?[10] Be that as it may, it is worth reiterating that there would be no GATT issue unless there is a link to discrimination against imported products.

*Article XI*

Article XI prohibits governmental use of most quantitative import and export restrictions and prohibitions. As such it does not discipline purely private actions or measures, although a question of some potential interest is whether there are any possible implications of this discipline for how certain private practices are treated.

In this regard, it may be interesting to consider reasoning used in a past dispute settlement case under GATT 1947. In the 1988 Panel Report on Japanese Trade in Semi-conductors,[11] the Panel found that Article XI measures were applied even though they did not have the status of being legally binding. In reaching this finding the Panel noted, *inter alia*, that:

"any measure instituted or maintained by a contracting party which restricted the exportation or sale for export of products was covered by this provision, irrespective of the legal status of the measure."

In this particular case, the Panel concluded that the absence of formally legally binding obligations in respect of exportation "amounted to a difference in form rather than substance because the measures were operated in a manner equivalent to mandatory requirements."

In reaching this finding the Panel had taken the view that it needed to be satisfied on two essential criteria:

> "First, there were reasonable grounds to believe that sufficient incentives or disincentives existed for non-mandatory measures to take effect. Second the operation of measures to restrict export...was essentially dependent on Government action or intervention."

This may raise the more general question of what kind of measures, short of formal legislation, would be sufficient to amount to an export restriction under Article XI.

*Article XVII*

This article on State-Trading Enterprises, imposes certain obligations with respect to the conduct of enterprises that are either state-*owned* or state-*controlled* or have been granted by the state "exclusive or special privileges."[12] The possible application of the GATS to such sectors is discussed below. The 1989 Panel Report on Korean Beef considered the scope of Article XVII. The Panel took the view that as the GATT did not concern the organisation and management of import monopolies but only their operations and effects on trade, the existence of a producer-controlled monopoly could not in itself be in violation of the GATT 1947.

With respect to state trading enterprises so defined, Article XVII requires that purchase and sales, including exports and imports should be made "in accordance with commercial considerations",[13] moreover, other Contracting Parties should be afforded "adequate opportunity to compete for participation in such purchases and sales".

Although the relationship of Article XVII to other GATT provisions has been considered by several Panels,[14] no Panel has ever found measures in violation of Article XVII itself. In the case of the national treatment issue, for instance, the 1992 *Beer* Panel Report went even further in considering the applicability of Article III:4 to a government monopoly for the distribution of alcoholic drinks. The Panel stated that it:

> "fully recognised that there was nothing in the General Agreement which prevented Canada from establishing import and sales monopolies that also had the sole right of internal delivery. The only

issue before the Panel was whether Canada, having decided to establish a monopoly for the internal delivery of beer, might exempt domestic beer from that monopoly. The Panel noted that Article III:4 did not differentiate between measures affecting the internal transportation of imported products that were imposed by governmental monopolies and those that were imposed in the form of regulations governing private trade.... Canada had the right to take, in respect of the privately delivered beer, the measures necessary to secure compliance with laws consistent with the General Agreement relating to the enforcement of monopolies. This right was specifically provided for in Article XX(d) of the General Agreement. The Panel recognised that a beer import monopoly that also enjoyed a sales monopoly might, in order properly to carry out its functions, also deliver beer but it did not for that purpose have to prohibit unconditionally the private delivery of imported beer while permitting that of domestic beer. For these reasons the Panel found that Canada's right ... did not entail the right to discriminate against imported beer inconsistently with Article III:4 through regulations affecting its internal transportation."

In the case of the 1989 Panel Report on Thailand - Restrictions on importation of and internal taxes on cigarettes the Panel stated that: "[t]he Thai Government may use (a governmental) monopoly to regulate the overall supply of cigarettes, their prices and their retail availability provided it thereby does not accord imported cigarettes less favourable treatment than domestic cigarettes or act inconsistently with any commitments assumed under its Schedule of Concessions." [15]

*Article XX(d)*

This article sets out the general exceptions to the GATT 1994. It provides that as long as governmental measures are not applied in a manner: (1) constituting a means of arbitrary or unjustifiable discrimination; or (2) a disguised restriction on international trade then WTO Members may adopt or enforce them where "necessary to secure compliance with laws or regulations which are not inconsistent with the provisions of this Agreement, including those relating to ... the enforcement of monopolies operated under (Articles II:4 and XVII ..."

The 1955 GATT Working Party on The Haitian Tobacco Monopoly [16] considered whether the licensing of tobacco imports by the local monopoly required a release under Article XVIII:12. The Panel concluded that Article XX(d) would be applicable to the measure if the basic regulations were not otherwise in conflict with any provisions of the GATT (1947). More recently, the 1988 Panel on Japanese Restrictions on Imports of Certain Agricultural Products[17] examined certain import quotas maintained by Japan. The Panel concluded that the enforcement of laws and regulations, providing for an import restriction made effective through an import monopoly inconsistent with Article XI:1 was not covered by the Article XX(d) exception. The 1992 *Beer* Panel limited the scope of the import monopoly to extend its market power to other areas. The Panel found that Canada had the right to take, in respect of the privately delivered beer, the measures necessary to secure compliance with laws consistent with the GATT 1947 relating to the enforcement of monopolies under Article XX(d). The Panel recognised that a beer import monopoly that also enjoyed a sales monopoly might, in order properly to carry out its functions, also deliver beer but it did not for that purpose have to prohibit unconditionally the private delivery of imported beer while permitting that of domestic beer.


*Article XXIII:1(b):*

The scope of governmental "measures" to which Article XXIII:1(b) may be deemed to apply was addressed in the 1998 Panel Report on Japanese Measures Affecting Consumer Photographic Film and Paper which considered the competitive relationship of the market place in considering the meaning of governmental "measures". The Panel also held the Government of Japan accountable for the actions of various private committees to which the government had delegated functions. With respect to governmental measures generally, the Panel stated that:

"In GATT jurisprudence, most of the cases of non-violation nullification or impairment have dealt with situations where a GATT-consistent domestic subsidy for the producer of a product has been introduced or modified following the grant of a tariff concession on that product. The instant case presents a different sort of non-violation claim. At the outset, however, we wish to make clear that we do not *a priori* consider it inappropriate to apply the Article XXIII:1(b) remedy to other governmental actions, such as those designed to strengthen the competitiveness of certain distribution or industrial sectors through non-financial assistance. Whether assistance is financial or non-financial, direct or indirect, does not determine whether its effect may offset the expected result of tariff negotiations. Thus, a Member's industrial policy, pursuing the goal of increasing efficiency in a sector, could in some circumstances upset the competitive relationship in the market place between domestic and imported products in a way that could give rise to a cause of action under Article XXIII:1(b). In the context of a Member's distribution system, for example, it is conceivable that measures that do not infringe GATT rules could be implemented in a manner that effectively results in a disproportionate impact on market conditions for imported products. In this regard, however, we must also bear in mind that tariff concessions have never been viewed as creating a guarantee of trade volumes, but rather, as explained below, as creating expectations as to competitive relationships."[18]


## Agreement on safeguards

The Preamble to the Safeguards Agreement states, *inter alia*, that members recognise "the importance of structural adjustment and the need to enhance rather than limit competition in international markets".

Article 11:1(b) provides that

"...a Member shall not seek, take or maintain any voluntary export restraints, orderly marketing arrangements or any other similar **measures on the export or the import side**."

The "similar measures" are specified to include:

"export moderation, export-price or import-price monitoring systems, export or import surveillance, compulsory import cartels and discretionary export or import licensing schemes, any of which afford protection" **to the importing country's industry**.

Furthermore, Article 11:3 provides that:

"Members shall not encourage or support the adoption or maintenance by public and private enterprises of non-governmental measures equivalent to those referred to in paragraph 1."

The question arises as to what would amount to "encouragement" or "support" by a government of, e.g. "export moderation" undertaken by private enterprises? Are these criteria different from, e.g. the criteria applicable in Article XI referred to above?

## General Agreement on Trade in Services (GATS)

The GATS contains a number of general obligations and disciplines that bind all Members irrespective of the specific commitments in their schedules with respect to particular services sectors, as well as general provisions on matters such as dispute settlement. In addition, the GATS also sets out a range of obligations that only apply to sectors in respect of which the Member in question has made specific commitments in its schedule. It is worth noting that GATS Article 1(3) covers "measures taken by non-governmental bodies in the exercise of [delegated] powers."

In the case of the general obligations and disciplines, binding on all Members irrespective of specific commitments, Articles 7 ("Recognition"), 8 ("Monopolies and Exclusive Service Suppliers") and 9 (Business Practices") contain a number of competition-related provisions. Articles 7 and 3 on Domestic Regulation and Transparency may also be relevant.

Article 7 has the apparent objective of preventing the use of licensing, certification or related requirements as a barrier to entry for foreign providers. The Article *permits* recognition of another Member's licensing or certification on a bilateral or plurilateral basis provided that "adequate opportunity" is afforded to other Members to negotiate their accession, and that the arrangements are not used as a means of discrimination between countries. Article 7 also states that "wherever appropriate" multilaterally agreed criteria are to be employed for recognition and harmonisation of these requirements.

Article 8 requires that monopolies whether public or private respect, *inter alia*, the Most-Favoured-Nation obligation in Article 2 of the GATS. In addition, with respect to sectors covered in a Member's schedule, Article 8 requires the Member to ensure that a monopoly supplier does not "abuse its monopoly position" when it competes in the supply of services outside its monopoly rights.

Article 9(1) provides that "Members recognise that certain business practices of service providers, other than those falling under Article 8, may restrain competition and thereby restrict trade in services." Article 9 obliges Members to accede to any request for consultation with any other Member concerning such practices "with a view to eliminating" them. It also imposes a duty to co-operate in the provision of non-confidential information of relevance to the matter in question.

## Understanding on commitments in financial services

The "Understanding on Commitments in Financial Services" sets out a framework, supplementing that of the main GATS text, on the basis of which Members have made specific commitments, in their schedules, with respect to measures on financial services. This Understanding contains a number of competition-related provisions:

- Paragraph 1 requires each member to list in its schedule existing monopoly rights; members "shall endeavour to eliminate ... or reduce" the scope of such rights.

- Paragraph 10.1 states that each Member "shall endeavour to remove or to limit any adverse effects" on other Members of a range of non-discriminatory measures, including restrictions on the range of services a given entity may provide, territorial limits on expansion into the entire territory of the Member, and, very generally, "other measures that ... affect adversely the ability of financial service suppliers of any other Member to operate compete or enter the Member's market".

- Paragraph 10.2 obligates Members to ensure that self-regulatory bodies, securities or other exchanges or markets, "or any other organisation or association" accord national treatment to foreign financial service providers, whenever membership in these bodies is *required* in order to deliver financial services within the Member state in question.

## Annex on telecommunications

The Annex contains an obligation to allow service providers of other Members access to public telecommunications networks "on reasonable and non-discriminatory terms and conditions" for the supply of any service included in the Member's schedule. This includes access to private leased circuits.

## Reference paper on basic telecommunications

The reference paper contains a general commitment of Members to maintain adequate measures to prevent anti-competitive practices of major suppliers.[19] In addition, it gives several specific examples of anti-competitive practices. These are:

- Anti-competitive cross-subsidisation.

- Use of information obtained from competitors.

- Withholding technical and commercial information.

Although not defined, anti-competitive cross-subsidisation would presumably occur if a service supplier or group of service suppliers that have market power, under the Reference Paper's definition of a "major supplier" were to use the supranormal profits, or rents, it gains from that segment to sustain a loss-making operation in a segment of the market where competition exists.

With respect to the broader concern of securing effective market access, the most important provisions in the reference paper are arguably those on interconnection with networks of major suppliers. Such interconnections are essential to competition, because otherwise the customers of one supplier cannot communicate with those of others. As Bronckers and Larouche note, "in large part, [these provisions] also seek to prevent anti-competitive behaviour by a major supplier..."[20] Essentially, interconnection must be on terms, conditions and rates that are "non-discriminatory" and the quality "no less favourable" than provided to subsidiaries, affiliates or third parties. Where there is a disagreement between a major supplier and a foreign provider on the terms, conditions or rates for interconnection, dispute settlement is mandated.

### Agreement on Trade-Related Intellectual Property Rights (TRIPS)

Article 8 provides that:

"Appropriate measures, provided they are consistent with the provisions of this Agreement, may be needed to prevent the abuse of intellectual property rights by rights holders or the resort to practices which unreasonably restrain trade or adversely affect the international transfer of technology."

The language "provided they are consistent with this Agreement" may be interpreted to mean that Article 8 is not a blanket limitation or exception clause. Rather, it may be interpreted as confirming that the potential bases for any actions to prevent abuse of intellectual property rights are to be those specifically provided for under other provisions of the Agreement, for example compulsory licensing of patents.

In addition, Article 40(1) recognises that that some licensing practices or conditions pertaining to intellectual property rights which restrain competition may have adverse effects on trade and may impede the transfer and dissemination of technology. Furthermore, Article 40(2) provides that nothing in the TRIPs Agreement shall prevent Members from specifying in their legislation licensing practices or conditions that may in particular cases constitute an abuse of intellectual property rights having an adverse effect on competition in the relevant market. Moreover, a Member may adopt appropriate measures to prevent or control such practices, which may include for example exclusive grantback conditions, conditions preventing challenges to validity and coercive package licensing.

In the case of trademarks, the owner's right to prohibit unauthorised use is limited to cases where the use "would result in a likelihood of confusion." However, where an identical sign is used "for identical goods and services", the likelihood of confusion is to be presumed. This raises the question of whether, in that case, the assumption is rebuttable. In general, the limitation of protected rights to where confusion exists reflects the underlying fair competition and consumer protection rationales for protecting marks.

In the case of geographical indications as well (Article 22), the rights which Members must guarantee related to prevention of use of indications "in a manner which misleads the public" or "constitutes an act of unfair competition" within the meaning of the *Paris Convention*. Some additional protections must be provided in the case of wine and spirits.

With respect to patents, compulsory licensing is explicitly contemplated as a remedy, including where [Article 31(k)] an anti-competitive practice has been determined to have occurred. The conditions of compulsory licensing in this circumstance are less onerous than otherwise (for example the license need not be non-exclusive, nor authorised predominantly for the supply of the Party's domestic market). Furthermore, "the need to correct anti-competitive practices may be taken into account in determining the amount of remuneration [to the patent holder] in such cases"...

## Other provisions[21]

- The Agreement on Technical Barriers to Trade includes rules to ensure that the preparation, adoption and application of technical regulations, standards and conformity assessment procedures *by non-governmental bodies* are not more trade restrictive than necessary (e.g. Articles 3,4,8).

- The Agreement on Preshipment Inspection includes detailed rules for the activities of *preshipment inspection entities* (Article 2).

- The Agreement on Subsidies regulates "market displacement", "price undercutting" and "voluntary undertakings" by exporters in detail (Articles 6,18) and explicitly requires the examination of "trade restrictive practices and competition between foreign and domestic producers" in determinations of "injury" (Article 15).

- What may be interpreted to be competition policy rationales may be invoked for other provisions/agreements. For example dumping, which is "condemned" under Article VI, and against which anti-dumping duties may be imposed subject to conditions defined in the Agreement Implementation of Article VI of the GATT 1994, may reflect, in some instances, a strategy of predatory pricing.

- The concept of non-violation nullification and impairment, based on Article XXIII of the GATT, may provide a basis to challenge denials of market access that fundamentally undermine bargained concessions. It has been argued that it is not precluded that restrictive business parties could be a factor in such situations.

- The Agreement on Trade-Related Investment Measures provides for a review by the Council for Trade in Goods of its operation not later than five years after the entry into force of the WTO Agreement. In the course of this review. "The Council for Trade in Goods shall consider whether the Agreement should be complemented with provisions on investment policy and competition policy."

- The Agreement on Government Procurement also might be relevant when it comes to certain anti-competitive private practices - for instance, by requiring transparency in government procurement decisions.


## Conclusions

The above survey of provisions in the WTO Agreements is not exhaustive either in descriptive or in analytic terms. However, it does suggest that the WTO Agreements do in fact deal to some extent with the trade and competition interface. The more interesting questions, it is suggested, are (a) how far does that coverage actually (or potentially) extend: and (b) is it necessary or desirable for this to be rationalised or clarified in a more coherent way and/or extended further.

This paper does not attempt to deal with the second question except to the extent that the exercise of reflection on what is or may be there already may shape one's view on the question of "what is to be done". Rather, the paper limits itself to the former question. Of course, it is for WTO Members themselves to interpret the rights and obligations under those Agreements. The object of this paper has been essentially to act as an aid to reflection by occasioning certain questions that may (or may not) be considered relevant to the matter at hand.

# NOTES

1.     See for instance, M.J. Trebilcock (1998), "Competition Policy and Trade Policy: Mediating the Interface" in R. Howse, ed., *The World Trading System: Critical Perspectives on the World Economy Vol. IV The Uruguay Round and Beyond,* Routledge: London, pp. 352-391.

2.     BISD 35S/37.

3.     BISD 39S/27.

4.     BISD 36S/268.

5.     BISD 34S/136.

6.     Findings at para 10.20 (WT/DS44/R 31, March 1998) Panel Report Adopted 22 April 1998.

7.     Ibid at para 10.380-10.382.

8.     L/833 adopted 23 October 1958.

9.     BISD 36S/345.

10.     Moving beyond this hypothetical situation, some authors (Bacchetta *et. al,* "Do negative spillovers from nationally pursued competition policies provide a case for Multilateral competition rules?" Paper presented at the Florence Conference on Competition Policy, June 13-14 1997, revised and unpublished August 1997) have suggested that the reach of this obligation could extend even further.

11.     BISD 35S/116.

12.     While Article XVII applies to trade in goods, not services, it is worth noting that in many countries, state trading enterprises might include enterprises in sectors like broadcasting, telecommunications, and financial services where entities typically have to acquire a license or charter and conform to a variety

of regulatory requirements in order to carry on business in the sector in question.

13. The 1984 Panel Report on the Canadian Administration of the Foreign Investment Review Act (FIRA) BISD 30S/140 considered the way in which the terms "commercial considerations" should be considered in the context of this Article. The Panel stated that: "the Panel considers that the commercial considerations criterion becomes relevant only after it has been determined that the governmental action at issue falls within the scope of the general principles of non-discriminatory treatment prescribed by the General Agreement."

14. FIRA, Supra note 14 at 40, para. 5.16; Canadian Import, Distribution and Sale of Alcoholic Drinks by Canadian Provincial Marketing Agencies, Supra note 2; and *Beer*, Supra note 3.

15. BISD 37S/200.

16. L/454, adopted on 22 November 1955, BISD 4S/38.

17. BISD 35S/163.

18. Ibid at 10.38.

19. A major supplier is defined as one with the power "to materially affect the terms of participation (having regard to price and supply", either due to control over essential, network facilities or its market position. This would most frequently the case with a former monopolist, whether public or private.

20. M.C.E.J. Bronckers and Pl Larouche (1997), "Telecommunications Services and the World Trade Organization", *31 Journal of World Trade 5*, p. 28.

21. See also Petersmann, "Competition Policy Aspects of the Uruguay Round: Achievements and Prospects"

*Chapter 5*

# IMPLICATIONS OF THE WTO AGREEMENT ON BASIC TELECOMMUNICATIONS

## Introduction

This paper discusses the implications of the GATS Agreement on Basic Telecommunications (the "ABT) for thinking about the relationship between trade and competition policies. The first section summarises the ABT. The second section introduces the Reference Paper to the ABT. The third section focuses on the factors facilitating the ABT and draws out certain insights for the future architecture of policies that aim to improve the coherence between trade and competition policies. The final section concludes that the ABT and Reference Paper are useful models for addressing that coherence in certain other sectors, but that this should be approached with appropriate caution.

## I.      GATS Basic Telecommunications Agreement: Summary[1]

The negotiations on basic telecommunications were not completed by the time the Uruguay Round drew to a close in December 1993. It had become apparent as the Uruguay Round negotiations on services proceeded that governments saw telecommunications as special because of their importance in the supply of many other services. Without access to telecom services, many other services cannot be delivered, making specific commitments in relation to the latter of dubious value. Thus, paragraph 5(a) of the GATS Annex on Telecommunications states that: "[e]ach Member shall ensure that any service supplier of any other Member is accorded access to and use of public telecommunications transport networks and services on reasonable and non-discriminatory terms and conditions for the supply of a service included in its Schedule.[2]

Suppliers of such services are entitled to access to and use of any public telecommunications transport network or service offered within or across the border, including private leased circuits, the right to purchase or lease and attach terminal or other equipment to the network, and to interconnect private leased or owned circuits with public telecommunications transport networks and services, or with circuits leased or owned by another service supplier. These rights are qualified by the right of the entity owning and/or controlling the network to impose conditions on access and use in order to safeguard public service responsibilities, protect the technical integrity of the networks or services, and to restrict network use where this is not required pursuant to a scheduled commitment. The obligations of the Annex extend not only to service suppliers in other sectors, but also to those in the telecommunications sector who would compete with incumbent network operators.[3]

Thus to a degree, competition policy-related issues concerning interconnection, market conduct safeguards, and transparency had already been touched upon in the GATS and its associated Annex on Telecommunications. However, some negotiators felt that the Annex commitments were too general to guarantee new entrants adequate opportunity to compete.

The obligations of GATS and the Annex on Telecommunications apply only to those telecommunications sectors that the WTO Members incorporated in their Schedules. Mostly, the Schedules contained what is commonly referred to as "enhanced telecommunications services." Enhanced services are those services in which the voice or nonvoice information being transferred from one point to another undergoes an end-to-end restructuring or format change before it reaches the customer. In 1994, the Members' Schedules generally included enhanced services, such as electronic mail, voice mail, on-line information, electronic data interchange, value-added facsimile services, code and protocol conversion, and data processing.

The Members were not ready in 1994 to make commitments on "basic telecommunications services" because, unlike enhanced services, the supply of basic services has been by state-owned operators or state-sanctioned monopolies. Thus, it became increasingly apparent that if negotiations were limited to the traditional trade approach of scheduling commitments on market access and national treatment, there would not be a guarantee that liberalisation commitments would translate into effective access to markets.[4] The removal of regulatory entry barriers is clearly a necessary condition of access, but such action would have little impact in the face of non-governmental barriers based on the ability of regulated incumbent firms to frustrate market entry.

Thus, a significant component of the extended negotiations centred around a quest for a set of acceptable regulatory principles that would be enforceable through WTO dispute settlement procedures. Accordingly, proposals were made to define interconnection rights more specifically. Market conduct safeguards were also sought to ensure that suppliers with market power refrain from a range of anti-competitive practices. Finally, transparency requirements were sought in order to ensure the availability of all information necessary for prompt and trouble-free interconnection.

The discussion of regulatory principles in the WTO negotiations revealed a preference among governments for a sector-specific approach over a more horizontal approach based on general rules. In part, this choice was due to the limited nature of the general competition law disciplines in the GATS. With respect to sectors covered in a Member's schedule, GATS Article VIII requires the Member to ensure that a monopoly supplier does not "abuse its monopoly position" when it competes in the supply of services outside its monopoly rights. Article IX:1 provides that "Members recognise that certain business practices of service providers, other than those falling under Article VIII, may restrain competition and thereby restrict trade in services." Article IX:2 obliges Members to accede to any request for consultation with any other Member concerning such practices "with a view to eliminating" them. It also imposes a duty to co-operate in the provision of non-confidential information of relevance to the matter in question.[5]

During most of the extended negotiations, regulatory principles were discussed exclusively in terms of protecting the interests of new market entrants against possible abuse of dominant position by incumbents. However, towards the end of the negotiations the problem of "one-way bypass" in international telecom services was raised. Concern was expressed that the interests of incumbents needed to be protected against potential predation by foreign entrants with dominant positions in their home markets. Thus, a proposal was made, for a licensing criterion designed to protect the conditions of competition in the domestic ("importing") market.

To summarise, at the conclusion of the negotiations, for each Member that participated in the continued negotiations, the following apply to its basic telecommunications services sectors: the obligations of GATS 1994, the 1994 Annex on Telecommunications; any 1997 limitations to MFN for basic telecommunications that it annexed to its 1994 List of Article II Exemptions; any 1997 commitments or limitations on market access and national treatment for basic telecommunications that it annexed to its 1994 Schedule of Specific

Commitments; any additional commitments made in its 1997 Schedule; and the commitments described in the Reference Paper for those countries that adopted it. We turn next to a consideration of the Reference Paper.

## II.    Reference Paper

The Reference Paper to the GATS Agreement on Basic Telecommunications Agreement (Reference Paper) represents a prominent example of a framework in a WTO agreement that already involves competition principles. Specifically, the Reference Paper contains a general commitment of Members to maintain appropriate measures to prevent suppliers unilaterally, or collectively, from engaging in or continuing anti-competitive practices. A "major supplier" is defined as one with the power "to materially affect the terms of participation (having regard to price and supply)", either due to control over essential, facilities or its market position.

In addition, the Reference Paper gives several specific examples of anti-competitive practices. These are:

- anti-competitive cross-subsidisation;

- use of information obtained from competitors (with "anti-competitive results"); and

- withholding technical and commercially relevant information.

The Reference Paper also applies to "interconnection" issues: e.g. the linking with suppliers providing public telecommunications transport networks or services to allow the users of one supplier to communicate with users of another supplier and to access services provided by another supplier. However, the extent of this obligation is limited to the specific commitments undertaken by a Member in the various schedules of GATS and ABT commitments. Interconnection must be provided:

- under non-discriminatory terms, conditions (including technical standards and specifications) and rates and of a quality no less favourable than that provided for its own like services or for like services of non-affiliated service suppliers or for its subsidiaries or other affiliates;

- in a timely fashion, on terms, conditions (including technical standards and specifications) and cost-oriented rates that are transparent, reasonable, having regard to economic feasibility, and sufficiently unbundled so that the supplier need not pay for network components or facilities that it does not require for the service to be provided; and

- upon request, at points in addition to the network termination points offered to the majority of users, subject to charges that reflect the cost of construction of necessary additional facilities.

The Reference Paper also builds on transparency in order to ensure that the Agreement can actually be operationalized. The procedures applicable for interconnection to a major supplier will be made publicly available, and a major supplier must make publicly available either its interconnection agreements or a reference interconnection offer.

With respect to settlement of disputes under the Agreement, the Reference Paper appears to distinguish between disputes about anti-competitive practices and disputes about interconnection. There is no particular form of dispute settlement provided for disputes over anti-competitive practices of major suppliers. However, a Reference Paper Signatory's failure to maintain appropriate measures to address anti-competitive conduct could, itself, be subject of dispute settlement. With respect to interconnection, the Reference Paper indicates that for dispute settlement, recourse is to be made to an independent domestic body. A service supplier requesting interconnection with a major supplier will have recourse, either: "at any time" or "after a reasonable period of time which has been made publicly known" to an independent domestic body, which may be a regulatory body.[6] That body must be given the authority to resolve disputes regarding appropriate terms, conditions and rates for interconnection within a reasonable period of time, to the extent that these have not been established previously. It is conceivable (and not precluded by the terms of the Reference Paper itself) that, the body might not be a sector-specific regulator, but e.g. a competition authority.

The Reference Paper also reflects a balance between the objectives of both trade liberalisation and competition policy and other social or policy objectives of interest to governments and civil society. The third commitment in the Reference Paper provides that any Member has the right to define the kind of universal service obligation it wishes to maintain, and such obligations will not be regarded as anti-competitive *per se*. However, those requirements must be administered in a transparent, non-discriminatory and competitively neutral manner and cannot be more burdensome than necessary for the kind of universal service defined by the Member. Similarly, any procedures for the allocation and use of scarce resources, including frequencies, numbers and rights of way, must be carried out in an objective, timely, transparent and non-discriminatory manner.

When the ABT entered into force in February 1998, 69 of the 130 WTO members committed to some degree of liberalisation of their telecommunication markets. Of these, 44 (representing 99% of basic telecommunications revenue among WTO members) permitted entry by foreign carriers. Furthermore, 55 countries agreed to adhere to the Reference Paper.[7]

## III.    Implications of the Agreement on Basic Telecommunications

In this section, we discuss the implications of the ABT for future multilateral rule-making with respect to trade and competition policy issues. First, we identify several unique factors that, in part, made possible this sectoral agreement. Second, we discuss possible ways in which the architecture of this agreement may be applied in other sectoral contexts, or to other multilateral rule making. Finally, we conclude with a discussion of several normative caveats, which suggest that this model should be invoked with some caution when it comes to other contexts.

### Factors Facilitating the ABT

First, over the last two decades and more there has been a spurt in technological developments in the telecommunications industry globally.[8] These developments on the supply-side have been matched with tremendous growth in demand for traditional and new forms of telecommunication services.

Second, this growth in demand is linked, in part, to the fact that telecommunication services are an important component of, or input into, traded or tradable services. The demand and supply of enhanced services and growth of foreign service suppliers in these areas have also tended to highlight the further gains that could be achieved by liberalisation of basic telecommunications services as well. Furthermore, as barriers between nations decline, and economic interdependence grows so to does the demand for increased links between national telecommunication networks. Consequently, this interdependence highlighted the need for a multilateral as opposed to a network of bilateral approaches. Furthermore, given the prominence of this sector in the modern global economy, certain growth-oriented developing countries may have chosen to signal their commitment to open trade and investment policies by agreeing to liberalisation in this sector.[9]

84

Third, over the same time period many of the leading markets for the demand and supply of telecommunications services have unilaterally liberalised their regulations of first, enhanced telecommunication services, and then basic telecommunication services. This liberalisation has in some cases also involved significant privatisation of incumbent domestic monopolies. This trend has been accompanied by increasing application of competition principles by telecommunications regulators, or in some cases the application of competition policy to these sectors.[10] There was wide agreement among Delegations that this transitional nature of the telecommunications industry from a highly regulated character with public monopolies to a less regulated character with more entrants and service providers was a crucial and unique feature recognition of which helps to explain the competition provisions of the Reference Paper. Once governments had decided to emphasise entry and to open this network industry to international competition, there was a feeling that traditional trade approaches to market access through national treatment and MFN commitments alone would not be sufficient to ensure successful entry by foreign service suppliers without additional competitive safeguards. Hence the Reference Paper builds on both traditional market access concepts as well as competition principles. Some Delegations noted that, in this respect, the Reference Paper could be seen as going beyond the existing approaches to access to "essential facilities" under the competition laws of many countries.

Fourth, the successful negotiation of the ABT may have something to do with the inherent character of trade in services as compared to trade in goods. It may be that trade in services is seen as inherently implicating "behind the border" domestic regulation to a much greater degree than the traditional "at the border" tariff or non-tariff barriers emphasis of the liberalisation of trade in goods. Even where the national treatment commitment applies behind the border to imported "like" products, it is less likely to call into question the existing domestic regulatory scheme and choices as appears to be the case in trade in many services. Accordingly, nations have been more hesitant to apply the broad traditional approach to applying the most-favoured-nation ("MFN") and national treatment principles than has been the case with trade in goods.

Therefore, from a pragmatic viewpoint, a negotiating approach based on a degree of up front liberalisation, and disciplines on domestic regulation may have been important. It may be that, for this reason, trade liberalisation and competition law and policy can act in a particularly focused and complementary fashion to promote pro-competitive reform of existing domestic regulation. While competition authorities will be concerned with promoting competition within the domestic market, trade officials will also be concerned with the relationship between the domestic market regulation, and export and foreign investment opportunities of domestic firms.

These four factors may not be necessary, but rather sufficient conditions, for trade and competition policy to work in a complementary fashion in respect of multilateral rule making. Accordingly, one might suggest that other highly regulated tradable service sectors characterised by network effects (e.g. electricity) may be candidates for the ABT approach to multilateral rule making. We will return to this point below.

## *Architecture*

Although the ABT is a sectoral agreement with respect to trade in services, its architecture might have implications for both trade in goods, and more general multilateral competition rule making. As discussed above, the ABT builds on the GATS commitment of: MFN and national treatment linked to schedules of commitments; transparency; disciplines on the abuse of a monopoly position by a monopoly supplier; and multilateral dispute settlement. In addition the ABT incorporates the Telecommunications Annex to the GATS which addresses issues of access and use of public telecommunications transport networks and services. Similarly, the ABT incorporates the Reference Paper; at least insofar as concerns the 55 countries that have agreed to adhere to it. The Reference Paper also addresses issues of anti-competitive practices and interconnection.

It may be worth giving further consideration to this aspect of the Reference Paper. As discussed above, the Reference Paper defines a "major supplier" as a supplier that has a material effect on price or quantity by virtue of controlling an essential facility or using its market position. No further definition is given of the term "essential facility" suggesting that each jurisdiction has, at least, some degree of regulatory flexibility. With respect to the major supplier's abuse of its market position, more guidance is given by a non-exhaustive list of anti-competitive practices - cross-subsidisation; the misuse of competitors' confidential information (presumably obtained from interconnection or through horizontal collusion); and withholding important information relating to an essential facility. In the context of the application of competition policy in most OECD Members, at least as regards telecommunications, this list is probably uncontroversial insofar as it goes. However, what is important here is that Members have agreed to a framework for thinking about anti-competitive practices in the telecommunications area while retaining important degrees of freedom to implement their regulatory policy choices. This point holds true even with respect to interconnection issues discussed in the Reference Paper. Again, if there were a failure to meet this obligation prematurely this would likely be a matter for multilateral dispute settlement.

Thus, the Reference Paper provides a flexible approach to dealing with certain trade and competition concerns. This flexible architecture is also manifested in the dispute settlement provisions of the Reference Paper. Countries have an obligation to maintain "appropriate measures" to prevent major suppliers from engaging or continuing to engage in anti-competitive practices. There is no obligation with respect to the detailed application of those laws. However, the WTO dispute settlement provisions could address the issue of whether a particular measure is "appropriate" without making a judgement about the application of the measure in any particular case. With respect to interconnection issues, countries are required to provide access to an independent "regulator", and such regulator is subject to certain other procedural requirements.

There was general agreement among Delegations that the ABT was facilitated by unique sectoral characteristics of that particular industry in transition. While many suggested that other sectors (e.g. electricity) characterised by network economies might also be candidates for an approach similar to that taken in the ABT, most Delegations cautioned that such an approach would not be a substitute for a horizontal approach to competition law in respect of any future multilateral rule-making. That being said, there was agreement among Delegations that some of the concepts and approaches in the ABT might also have relevance to further thinking about such multilateral rule-making. In that regard, a Delegation noted that in applying the ABT some countries would choose to rely on their domestic telecommunications regulators rather than their competition authorities. That Delegation also noted that in the ongoing discussions around the "built in" GATS negotiating agenda, there appears to be some interest in further exploring the application of competition principles to constrain anti-competitive distortions that may be sometimes facilitated by domestic regulations and regulators. By contrast, the ABT permits countries to rely on the domestic regulators to enforce the competitive safeguards to facilitate entry and market access.

*Caveats*

Three important caveats about the ABT model of dealing with trade and competition concerns can be identified at this stage. First, it might be argued that if governments agree to create mutual obligations to enforce a given set of regulatory principles, they could be viewed as having tied themselves into an established pattern of regulation. This approach may be appealing from the point of view of opening up market access on a broadly reciprocal basis. However, it also has the potential drawback of locking in a uniform approach in circumstances that might be quite different among countries. In the specific context of the ABT and the Reference Paper, and the more general context of possible future multilateral initiatives that might build upon the flexible architecture described above, this will not necessarily be the case. That is so because the Reference Paper does not set forth a detailed or mechanical "common standard" for regulation of the telecommunications sector. Rather, the Reference Paper provides an approach to applying principles of competition to the telecommunications sector while leaving significant freedom and flexibility for Members to implement their regulatory policy choices.

This problem, to the extent that it exists, can also be addressed through the design of the regulatory principles that do not apply when a given threshold of diversification in relation to the sources of supply available in a market has been attained. Even so, multilateral uniformity may still in some circumstances lead to a suboptimal degree of regulatory intervention. In other words, the regulatory authorities, or the governments, to whom they are ultimately responsible, could find that multilateral commitments make regulatory forbearance harder in circumstances where it might otherwise seem desirable. Again, for the reasons described above, in the specific context of the ABT and the Reference Paper, and the more general context of possible future multilateral initiatives that might build upon its flexible architecture, there is no *a priori* reason to expect this result to occur.

The third caveat is the risk that regulatory interventions putatively designed to promote competition instead become primarily used to protect competitors, not competition. However, given the flexible architecture of the ABT and the Reference Paper, there does not appear to be any *a priori* reason to expect the problem of rent seeking to be worsened by the multilateral agreement. On the contrary, the embodied emerging consensus among trade and competition officials about telecommunications regulation would seem to strengthen, rather than weaken the hands of those authorities wrestling with these forms of rent seeking behaviour. It must also be recognised that antitrust laws and their enforcement may, in certain jurisdictions - inside and outside the OECD - reflect multiple objectives, including industrial policy considerations. It is also true that antitrust authorities may be subject to the similar problems of capture and political influence as other types of regulators.

## Conclusions

This paper has attempted to set forth some of the implications of the ABT for multilateral rule making in respect of trade and competition policy issues, while recognising that there are discrete factors that led to the creation of what one commentator has called "a unique and slightly divergent method for the establishment of international competition".[11]  Where similar conditions are present, the ABT might provide a useful model for dealing with these issues in other sectors such as electricity.   However, such sectoral approaches are generally not seen as substitutes for a horizontal approach to competition law at either national or multilateral level.  Furthermore, there are important caveats that must be considered closely before generalising a sector-specific approached to regulation.   Nonetheless, the architecture of the ABT also provides an interesting model that might warrant closer scrutiny to see whether any of the principles, concepts and approaches might also be applicable to further multilateral rule-making in respect of anti-competitive practices that have a significant impact on international trade.

# NOTES

1.　　See generally: Marco C.E.J. Bronkers and Pierre Larouche, "Telecommunications Services and the World Trade Organization" *31 Journal of World Trade 5* (June 1997); and Bernard Hoekman, Patrick Low and Petros Mavroidis, "Regulation, Competition Policy and Market Access Negotiations: Lessons From the Telecommunications Sector" in Einar Hope (ed.), *Competition Policies for an Integrated World Economy* (Routledge, forthcoming).

2.　　Non-discrimination in this context comprises both MFN and national treatment.

3.　　It should be noted that Annex commitments only apply in those sectors where governments have accepted specific market access and national treatment commitments. Under the GATS, governments have negotiated these commitments on a sector-by-sector basis, and in sectors that are not covered in this manner, the only obligations that apply relate to most-favoured-nation treatment and transparency.

4.　　Patrick Low, "Multilateral Rules on Competition: What Can We Learn From the Telecommunications Sector?," presented at an OECD workshop on Trade Policy for a Globalizing Economy, Santiago, Chile (November 1995).

5.　　See paper on "Competition Elements In International Trade Agreements: A Post-Uruguay Round Overview Of WTO Agreements".

6.　　In the case where this is a "regulatory body" it must be separate from, and not accountable to, any supplier of basic telecommunications services, and the decisions of and the procedures used by regulators must be impartial with respect to all market participants.

7.　　Toshiaki Takigawa, "The Impact of the WTO Telecommunications Agreement on U.S. and Japanese Telecommunications Regulations" *32 Journal of World Trade 33* (December, 1998) at 39-40. C.f. Lawrence J. Spiwak, "From International Competitive Carrier to the WTO: A Survey of the FCC's International Telecommunications Policy Initiatives 1985-1998" 51 Fed. Com. L.J. 111 (December 1998) at 176 noting that certain "of the signatory countries agreed to uphold certain 'pro-competitive regulatory principles' yet, at the same time, these signatory countries also condone those signatory countries which refuse to allow any new competitors to enter their market."

8.  See generally OECD *Information Technology Outlook 1997* (1997) and OECD *Communications Outlook 1997* (1997) at 31.

9.  Patrick Low and Aadityi Mattoo, "Reform in Basic Telecommunications and the WTO Negotiations: The Asian Experience", WTO Staff Working Paper ERAD9801 (February 1998) at 26.

10. See generally: OECD *Competition in Telecommunications* OCDE/GD(96)114 and OECD *Developments In Telecommunications: An Update Aide Memoire* (1997).

11. James F. Rill *et al.*, "Institutional Responsibilities Affecting Competition in the Telecommunications Industry: A Practicing Lawyer's Perspective" Working Draft Paper prepared for the European University Institute 1998 EU Competition Workshop at p. 23.

OECD PUBLICATIONS, 2, rue André-Pascal, 75775 PARIS CEDEX 16
PRINTED IN FRANCE
(22 1999 04 1 P) ISBN 92-64-17129-0 – No. 50905 1999